Chocolate

Crazy

SYLVIA BALSER HIRSCH

Macmillan Publishing Company
New York

Collier Macmillan Publishers
London

Macmillan Publishing Company
866 Third Avenue, New York, N.Y. 10022
Collier Macmillan Canada, Inc.

Library of Congress Cataloging in Publication Data

Hirsch, Sylvia Balser.
  Chocolate crazy.

  Includes index.
  1. Cookery (Chocolate)   I. Title.
TX767.C5H48   1984   641.6′374   84-14396
ISBN 0-02-551840-2

Macmillan books are available at special discounts
for bulk purchases for sales promotions, premiums,
fund-raising, or educational use. Special editions
or book excerpts can also be created to specifica-
tion. For details, contact:

  Special Sales Director
  Macmillan Publishing Company
  866 Third Avenue
  New York, New York 10022

10   9   8   7   6   5   4   3   2   1

Printed in the United States of America

In loving memory of the first "chocoholics" I ever knew—
my dear parents.

My thanks to all the nameless housewives who sent their family treasures in hopes of getting a Miss Grimble recipe.

Contents

Introduction

Enter my wonderful world of chocolate. My father said, "If it isn't chocolate, it isn't dessert!" He was not a demanding man and enjoyed everything presented but "sat his table" until a bit of chocolate was served with his coffee, if it had not been served as dessert. Mother was desperate enough at times to resort to squares of Hershey's chocolate candy bar! My father was a true chocoholic and as far as I am concerned coined the word before it was popularized. Mother would often ponder aloud, "What to serve for dessert?" and Father would always say, "When in doubt, serve chocolate." He was right— chocolate *is* "black magic."

Know Your Chocolate

Unsweetened chocolate or bitter chocolate is for baking or cooking. It is made without sugar.

Bittersweet or semisweet chocolate is slightly sweetened. It is used for desserts, frostings, fillings, candymaking, creams, sauces, and mousses.

Milk chocolate is a great favorite and found in most candy bars. It is also popularly used for cake frostings and fillings, pie fillings, puddings, and creams.

Cocoa powder includes several kinds. There is Dutch-process cocoa that has alkali added to neutralize the acidity. It is darker than regular unsweetened breakfast cocoa and has a different flavor. The more common cocoas include breakfast cocoa, which may or may not be sweetened.

Chocolate syrup, such as Hershey's, is sweetened and flavored. It is used in drinks, sauces, and some baking.

White chocolate is only called chocolate, as it is merely vegetable fat with only one component of chocolate—cocoa butter—flavored and sometimes colored. It is popular for dipping, mousses, and some frostings and fillings.

To substitute cocoa for chocolate—remember that 1 square of chocolate equals 3 tablespoons of cocoa plus $1\frac{1}{2}$ teaspoons of cocoa butter.

Cake Sizes and Servings

These are approximations, but they will serve as good guidelines.

8-inch square cake	serves 6–8
8-inch round cake—2–3 layers	serves 8–10
9-inch round cake—2–3 layers	serves 10–12
8-inch springform	serves 6–8
9-inch springform	serves 8–10
10-inch springform	serves 10–12
Tube pans	servings correspond to layer cakes in size
9 × 5 × 2¾-inch loaf pan	serves 12
13 × 9 × 2-inch pan	yields 24 2-inch squares

Filling and Frosting Guidelines

To Frost: **Use:**

9-inch cake layer, top and sides ¾ cup of frosting or filling

For each additional layer add ¾ cup of frosting or filling

9 × 5 × 2¾-inch cake top and sides 1½ cups of frosting or filling

If split into layers, add ½ cup of frosting or filling

10 × 15-inch cake roll 2 cups of frosting or filling

8-inch square cake, top and sides 1½–2 cups of frosting or filling

12 cupcakes 1½ cups of frosting or filling

And Remember:

All butter called for in these recipes should be salted butter. Unsalted or sweet butter will not give the desired result.

I believe the best results in beating egg whites come from using a very large open platter (21–25 inches) and a whisk, instead of a bowl. With this method, you get twice the volume of egg whites.

To enhance the flavor of cakes, dust the baking pan with cocoa instead of flour.

CHEESECAKES

Chocolate Chip Cheesecake
Chocolate Italian Cheesecake
Fudgey Cheesecake
Kahlua Cheesecake
Mocha Chocolate Cheesecake
Elegant Italian Cheese Roll

Chocolate Chip Cheesecake

9-inch springform pan, buttered

Crust:

1¼ cups chocolate wafer crumbs (about 22 chocolate
   wafers)
¼ cup (½ stick) butter, melted
1 tablespoon sugar

Filling:

5 packages (8 ounces each) cream cheese, softened
1¾ cups sugar
¼ cup all-purpose flour
1 teaspoon vanilla
5 eggs
2 egg yolks
½ cup semisweet mini-chocolate pieces
¼ cup heavy cream

Garnish:

Sweetened whipped cream cheese
Chocolate curls

Preheat oven to 450°F.

Combine wafer crumbs, butter, and the 1 tablespoon sugar in small
bowl. Press evenly over bottom and sides of pan. Refrigerate.

Beat together cream cheese, 1¾ cups sugar, 3 tablespoons of flour,
and vanilla in large bowl until smooth and fluffy. Beat in eggs and
yolks, one at a time, until mixture is well blended. Dust chocolate
pieces with 1 tablespoon flour. Stir chocolate pieces and heavy cream
into batter. Pour batter into pan. Place on cookie sheet.

Bake in preheated oven for 10 minutes. Lower oven temperature to
200°F, and bake 1 hour more. Turn off oven. Leave cake in unopened
oven 1 hour. Open oven door, leave cake in oven 30 minutes more.
Cool on wire rack to room temperature. (This cheesecake may crack
on top.) Refrigerate overnight.

To serve, remove cake from pan. Garnish with sweetened whipped
cream cheese rosettes and chocolate curls.

Serves 10–12.

Chocolate Italian Cheesecake

9-inch springform pan, buttered

Crust:

1 cup all-purpose flour

¼ cup sugar

1 teaspoon grated orange zest

¼ teaspoon vanilla

1 egg yolk

¼ pound sweet butter

2 tablespoons crème de cacao, chilled

Filling:

15 ounces whole milk ricotta cheese

½ cup sugar

¼ cup flour

4 eggs

¼ cup crème de cacao

3 tablespoons orange zest

Topping:

1 cup whipped cream, lightly sweetened

Bitter chocolate, grated

Preheat oven to 350°F.

Prepare dough by combining the flour, sugar, orange zest, and vanilla in a large bowl. Make a well in the center and add the egg yolk and butter. Work together quickly with a pastry blender. Add the chilled liqueur to bind the dough.

Wrap the dough in wax paper and chill thoroughly, at least 1 hour.

Roll dough to ⅛ inch thick and fit into bottom and sides of the springform pan. Bake in preheated oven for 15 minutes until dry. Remove from oven and cool. Reduce oven heat to 325°F.

To make the filling: Cream the cheese with the sugar and flour until smooth. Add the eggs, 1 at a time, beating after each addition until well blended. Add the liqueur and zest, mix well, and spoon into the cooled baked shell. Bake for 1 hour and 10 minutes.

Remove from oven and cool to room temperature before releasing sides of pan and serving. Garnish with cream and chocolate.

Serves 10.

Fudgey Cheesecake

For the cheesecake "maven" this is Nirvana attained!

9-inch springform pan, buttered

Crust:

1½ cups chocolate cookie crumbs
 6 tablespoons butter, melted
 ¼ cup sugar
 ⅛ teaspoon cinnamon

Filling:

1½ pounds cream cheese
 ⅔ cup sugar
 3 eggs
 2 teaspoons instant coffee
 2 teaspoons vanilla
 6 squares (6 ounces) bittersweet chocolate, melted and
    cooled
 1 cup heavy cream
    Confectioner's sugar

Preheat oven to 275°F.

To make the crust: In a bowl, combine the cookie crumbs, melted butter, sugar, and cinnamon until well blended. Press onto the bottom and sides of the prepared springform pan. Keep cool or chilled until filling is prepared.

To make the filling: In the bowl of an electric mixer, combine the cheese with the sugar and beat until smooth and creamy. Add the eggs, coffee, and vanilla, and continue to beat until well blended. Add the melted chocolate and heavy cream and stir until all the streaks are gone.

Pour the mixture into the prepared crust and bake for 1 hour and 15 minutes. Turn off the heat and cool the cake in the oven until the cake reaches room temperature. Chill for 3–4 hours before removing springform.

Serves 10–12.

Kahlua Cheesecake

What could be better than Kahlua and cocoa?

9-inch springform pan, buttered

Crust:

1½ cups chocolate cookie crumbs
⅓ cup butter, melted

Filling:

1 8-ounce package cream cheese, softened
¾ cup sugar
½ cup cocoa
2 eggs
5 tablespoons Kahlua
¼ cup extra-stong coffee
1 teaspoon vanilla

Topping:

1 cup whipping cream
2 tablespoons sugar
1 tablespoon Kahlua
Bitter chocolate, shaved

Preheat oven to 375°F.

Combine the cookie crumbs with the melted butter and pat gently onto the bottom and sides of the springform pan.

To make the filling: In the large bowl of an electric mixer, combine the cream cheese with the sugar and beat until light and thoroughly blended. Add the cocoa and eggs, and beat until well blended. Stir in the liqueur, coffee, and vanilla. Spoon the mixture into the prepared pan and bake in preheated oven for 25 minutes. Remove from oven and cool.

Chill 6–8 hours.

Remove the springform ring. Whip the cream with the sugar and Kahlua. Top the cake with the flavored whipped cream. Garnish with shaved bitter chocolate.

Serves 10–12.

Mocha Chocolate Cheesecake

During the infancy of the Grimble Bakery, this was a house specialty.

8-inch springform pan, buttered

Crust:
- ¾ cup chocolate cookie crumbs
- 4 tablespoons butter, melted
- 1½ tablespoons sugar

Filling:
- 3 8-ounce packages cream cheese
- 1 cup sugar
- 2 eggs
- 8 ounces semisweet chocolate bits
- 2 tablespoons heavy cream
- 1 cup sour cream
- ¼ cup extra-strong coffee
- 1 teaspoon vanilla
- ¼ cup dark rum

Topping:
- 1 tablespoon cocoa
- 1 tablespoon confectioner's sugar

Preheat oven to 350°F.

Blend together the cookie crumbs, butter, and sugar. Press onto the bottom and sides of the prepared springform pan. Cool or chill.

To make the filling: In the large bowl of an electric mixer, cream the cheese with the sugar, then add the eggs and blend.

Over very low heat, melt the chocolate with the heavy cream, then remove from the heat and add the sour cream, coffee, and vanilla and add to the cheese mixture, with rum, blending until smooth.

Pour into the prepared crust and bake in preheated oven for 45 minutes or until puffed at sides. Cool on a rack for 3–4 hours. Remove the springform and garnish by sprinkling or sifting the cocoa and confectioner's sugar over the top.

Serves 8–12.

Elegant Italian Cheese Roll

This is sheer sorcery! Serve it with a bowl of your favorite chocolate sauce spiked with a bit of rum.

---

      9 × 13-inch jelly-roll pan, buttered, lined with wax paper, and buttered

- 3 eggs, separated
- ½ cup confectioner's sugar, plus additional for garnish
- 1½ teaspoons vanilla
- 2 tablespoons flour, sifted
- 3 tablespoons cocoa
- ⅛ teaspoon salt
- ½ teaspoon cream of tartar
- 15 ounces whole milk ricotta cheese
- ¼ cup sugar
- 2 tablespoons dark rum
- 1½ tablespoons grated orange zest

Preheat oven to 325°F.

In the large bowl of an electric mixer, beat the egg yolks until lemony, then slowly add the ½ cup of confectioner's sugar and 1 teaspoon of vanilla, beating until creamy.

Resift the flour with the cocoa and the salt and blend into the egg mixture.

On a large open platter beat the egg whites with the cream of tartar until stiff but not dry, then fold into the cake batter. Spoon the batter evenly into the pan and bake in preheated oven for about 25 minutes.

Remove from the oven and let stand about 5 minutes, then turn out on a lightly dampened clean tea towel. Remove the paper and trim off the crisp edges of cake. Roll up the cake gently in the towel and set it aside to cool.

Beat the cheese with the sugar, rum, zest, and ½ teaspoon of vanilla until smooth.

Gently unroll the cake and spread with the cheese mixture. Reroll the cake and wrap it in wax paper. Chill in the refrigerator for several hours.

To serve, sprinkle with confectioner's sugar and pass a bowl of chocolate sauce with rum, such as the Simplest Ever Ice Cream Sauce (p. 184) or Hot Chocolate Sauce (p. 183), using rum instead of sherry.

Serves 10.

CAKES

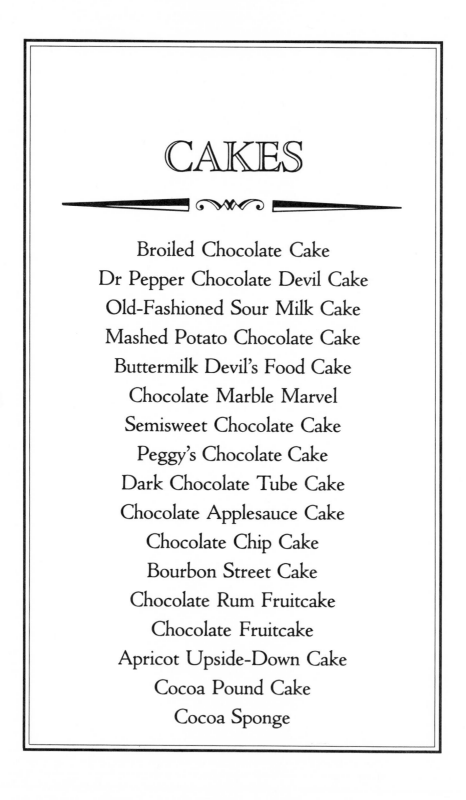

Broiled Chocolate Cake

Dr Pepper Chocolate Devil Cake

Old-Fashioned Sour Milk Cake

Mashed Potato Chocolate Cake

Buttermilk Devil's Food Cake

Chocolate Marble Marvel

Semisweet Chocolate Cake

Peggy's Chocolate Cake

Dark Chocolate Tube Cake

Chocolate Applesauce Cake

Chocolate Chip Cake

Bourbon Street Cake

Chocolate Rum Fruitcake

Chocolate Fruitcake

Apricot Upside-Down Cake

Cocoa Pound Cake

Cocoa Sponge

Company Sponge Roll

Passover Sponge Cake

Easy Whipped Cream Log

Chocolate Spice Roll

Chocolate Roll with Preserves

Rum Raisin Icebox Cake

Chocolate Delmonico Cake

Filled Chocolate Angel Food Cake

Sweet Chocolate Muffins

Cupcakes for Your Lovable
Little Ones

Broiled Chocolate Cake

This is a different taste experience.

9-inch square pan, lined with wax paper

     4 squares (4 ounces) sweet chocolate
  1½ cups cake flour, sifted
     1 cup sugar
    ½ teaspoon baking soda
    ½ teaspoon baking powder
    ½ teaspoon salt
  5½ tablespoons butter, softened
    ¾ cup buttermilk
     1 teaspoon vanilla
     2 eggs

Frosting:
     4 tablespoons butter, softened
    ⅔ cup grated coconut
    ½ cup packed brown sugar
    ¼ cup chopped walnuts
     2 tablespoons light cream

Preheat oven to 350°F.

In the top of a double boiler over hot but not boiling water, melt the chocolate. Cool.

Resift the flour with the dry ingredients.

Put the butter in the bowl of an electric mixer and add the flour mixture, ⅓ cup of the buttermilk, and the vanilla. Beat on medium for 2 minutes. Add the chocolate, eggs, and the remaining buttermilk. Beat 1 minute more and spoon into the prepared pan. Bake for about 40 minutes, until a toothpick inserted into the cake comes out clean.

Remove from oven and top with frosting while the cake is still hot.

To make the frosting: Blend together all the ingredients. Spread over the hot cake, then broil 3 inches from the heat, for about 3 minutes until bubbly and lightly brown. Cool sufficiently to remove from pan and serve slightly warm.

Serves 8.

Dr Pepper Chocolate Devil Cake

It is said that Texans brag! Well, here is another reason for bragging. The Dr Pepper drink originated in Texas. This cake was developed in their kitchen.

---

3 8-inch cake pans, buttered and lightly dusted with cocoa

1 stick butter or margarine
2½ cups packed light brown sugar
3 eggs
3 squares (3 ounces) bitter chocolate, melted
2¼ teaspoons baking soda
½ cup buttermilk
½ teaspoon salt
2¼ cups cake flour, sifted
2 teaspoons vanilla
1 cup Dr Pepper, heated to boiling

Preheat oven to 375°F.

Cream the butter or margarine. Add the brown sugar gradually, creaming until well blended. Add the eggs, 1 at a time, beating well after each addition. Add the melted chocolate that has been slightly cooled.

Add 1 teaspoon of baking soda to the buttermilk. Add 1¼ teaspoons of baking soda and the salt to the flour. Add the flour and the buttermilk alternately to the butter-sugar mixture, starting with the flour and ending with the flour. Add the vanilla and mix in the boiling Dr Pepper. (Do not be alarmed by the thinness of the batter after adding the boiling Dr Pepper.) Blend well.

Pour the batter equally into the prepared pans and bake in preheated oven for 25–30 minutes, until a toothpick inserted into the cake comes out clean. Cool on racks. Fill and frost with your favorite chocolate frosting, or see pages 42–45.

Serves 8–10.

Old-Fashioned Sour Milk Cake

Here's a cake that's an absolute joy!

---

2 8-inch cake pans, buttered and dusted with cocoa

½ cup vegetable shortening
1¼ cups sugar
½ teaspoon salt
1½ teaspoons vanilla
2 eggs
2 squares (2 ounces) bitter chocolate, melted
1¾ cups cake flour, sifted
1 teaspoon baking soda
1 cup sour milk

Frosting:
2 tablespoons water
¼ cup sugar
¼ teaspoon salt
2½ cups confectioner's sugar, sifted
1 egg
½ cup vegetable shortening
1 teaspoon vanilla
2 squares (2 ounces) bitter chocolate, melted

Preheat oven to 350°F.

To measure shortening for ½ cup, use a 1-cup measuring cup and fill it to ½ cup with water, then add the shortening to the full 1-cup measure.

To sour milk, add 1 tablespoon of lemon juice to fresh milk.

In the large bowl of an electric mixer, beat the shortening with the sugar, salt, vanilla, and eggs until light. Add the melted chocolate and continue to beat about 2–3 minutes.

Resift the sifted flour with the baking soda and add to the batter alternately with the sour milk, beating to blend.

Divide the batter equally and pour into the prepared pans. Bake for 30–35 minutes, until toothpick inserted into the cake comes out clean. Remove from the oven and let cool in pans about 10 minutes. Remove the layers from pans and cool completely on rack.

To make the frosting: In a saucepan, combine the water, sugar, and salt, bring to a boil, and let boil 1 minute. Remove from heat and gradually beat in the confectioner's sugar and egg. Add the shortening, vanilla, and melted chocolate, and beat until smooth and creamy.

Frost the cake when cool.

Serves 8–10.

Mashed Potato Chocolate Cake

Many cooks have added mashed potatoes to cakes for added moistness. Here's something a little different.

---

3 8-inch cake pans, buttered and lightly floured

3 squares (3 ounces) bittersweet chocolate, grated
⅔ cup milk, heated
1 cup hot mashed potatoes
2 sticks butter
2 cups sugar
1 teaspoon vanilla
2 cups flour
3 teaspoons baking powder
½ teaspoon salt
4 eggs, separated
¼ cup confectioner's sugar

Frosting:
2 squares (2 ounces) bitter chocolate
2 tablespoons butter, softened
½ teaspoon vanilla
    Pinch salt
1 cup confectioner's sugar
1 egg

Preheat oven to 350°F.

Combine the chocolate with the milk and stir until melted. Combine with the hot mashed potatoes.

Cream together the butter, sugar, and vanilla until smooth. Stir into the chocolate-potato mixture and blend.

Sift the flour with the baking powder and salt.

Beat the egg yolks and blend into the potato batter alternately with the flour mixture.

On a large open platter, beat the egg whites into soft peaks and gradually add the confectioner's sugar. Fold into the batter and spoon into the prepared pans.

Bake for 35–40 minutes, until a toothpick inserted into the cake comes out clean. Remove from oven and cool on rack for 5 minutes. Remove the layers from pans and cool on racks.

To make the frosting: In the top of a double boiler over hot but not boiling water, melt the chocolate with the butter, vanilla, and salt. When well blended, work in the confectioner's sugar gradually until smooth, then beat in the egg. Beat until thick and cool enough to spread.

Serves 8–10.

Buttermilk Devil's Food Cake

What cakes do Americans love most? Chocolate cakes, of course, and so do I.

---

   3   9-inch cake pans, buttered and lightly dusted with cocoa

   1   stick butter
2½   cups packed light brown sugar
   3   eggs
3½   squares (3½ ounces) bitter chocolate, melted
2¼   cups cake flour, sifted
   2   teaspoons baking soda
   ½   teaspoon salt
   ½   cup buttermilk
   1   cup boiling water
2¼   teaspoons vanilla

Sour Cream Frosting:
   3   cups bittersweet chocolate
1½   cups sour cream
1½   teaspoons vanilla
       Pinch salt

Preheat oven to 375°F.

In the large bowl of an electric mixer, cream the butter and slowly add the brown sugar, beating until mixture is smooth. Add the eggs, 1 at a time, beating well after each addition, then blend in the melted chocolate.

Resift the sifted cake flour with the baking soda and salt.

Add the flour mixture alternately with the buttermilk to the butter mixture and mix well.

Stir in the boiling water and vanilla, mix the batter well and pour into the prepared cake pans, dividing equally.

Bake in preheated oven for 25–30 minutes, until a toothpick inserted into the cake comes out clean. Remove from oven and cool for about 5 minutes before removing from pans.

To make the frosting: In the top of a double boiler over hot but not boiling water, melt the chocolate. Remove from heat and beat in the sour cream, vanilla, and salt. Beat until the frosting is creamy and holds its shape.

Fill and frost the completely cooled cake.

Serves 8–10.

Chocolate Marble Marvel

Need I say more?

---

2 8-inch square pans, buttered and dusted with cocoa

6 eggs
1 cup sugar
¾ cup flour, sifted
¼ cup cocoa
1 stick butter, melted and cooled
1½ teaspoons vanilla

Preheat oven to 350°F.

In the large bowl of an electric mixer, combine the eggs with the sugar and beat until lemony.

Set the bowl over hot water and heat over low heat, stirring until lukewarm. Place the bowl back under the mixer and beat on high for 15 minutes.

Pour half of the mixture into another bowl.

Sift ¼ cup of flour with the cocoa over half the batter, very lightly. Add 4 tablespoons of melted butter and blend.

To the other half of the batter, add remaining ½ cup of sifted flour gradually with remaining 4 tablespoons of melted butter and the vanilla.

When both batters are blended, pour each into a 2-cup measuring cup. While holding both cups in one hand, pour the batters in a swirling fashion into prepared pans and bake for 30 minutes, until a toothpick inserted into the cake comes out clean.

Invert cakes on racks, remove from pans, and cool.

Fill and frost with Crème Ganache (p. 43).

Serves 8–10.

Semisweet Chocolate Cake

A chocolate treasure.

---

    2 9-inch cake pans, buttered

    6 ounces semisweet chocolate bits
    ½ cup boiling water
    2 sticks butter
    2 cups sugar
    4 eggs, separated
    1 teaspoon vanilla
    2½ cups flour, sifted
    1 teaspoon baking soda
    ½ teaspoon salt
    1 cup buttermilk

Frosting:

    1 14-ounce can sweetened condensed milk
    4 tablespoons butter
    6 ounces semisweet chocolate bits
       Pinch salt
    1 teaspoon vanilla or Kahlua
    ½ cup chopped pecans

Preheat oven to 350°F.

In a saucepan, combine the chocolate and the water, and stir over low heat until melted and blended.

In the large bowl of an electric mixer, combine the butter and sugar, and beat until lemony. Add the egg yolks, 1 at a time, then the melted chocolate and the vanilla.

Sift all the dry ingredients together and add to the chocolate mixture alternately with the buttermilk.

On a large open platter, beat the egg whites until stiff but not dry and gently fold into the batter. Pour equally into the prepared cake pans and bake for 35–40 minutes, until a toothpick inserted into the cake comes out clean. Cool in pans.

To make the frosting: In a shallow saucepan, place the condensed milk and the butter and bring to a boil, stirring constantly, for about 1 minute. Remove from heat and add the chocolate bits and salt; stir until completely melted and blended. Add the vanilla or liqueur last. Let this frosting cool until the right consistency to spread.

Fill and frost the cake, then decorate the top with the chopped pecans.

Serves 10–12.

Peggy's Chocolate Cake

Peggy Solomon and I exchanged many recipes over the years I lived in Dallas. She is probably one of the best all-around hostesses among my group of friends. The following recipe was generously given to me years ago.

When I use this frosting, I fill the layers with raspberry jam.

---

2 9-inch cake pans, buttered

3 squares (3 ounces) bitter chocolate, grated
½ cup hot water
1 stick butter
1⅔ cups sugar
3 eggs
2 cups cake flour, sifted
½ teaspoon salt
¼ teaspoon baking soda
3 teaspoons baking powder
1 cup buttermilk
1 teaspoon vanilla

Fudge Frosting:
4 squares (4 ounces) bitter chocolate
2 cups sugar
1 cup light cream
1 teaspoon vanilla
½ cup raspberry jam

Preheat oven to 350°F.

In a small saucepan, combine the grated chocolate with the hot water and cook to a thick paste, stirring constantly, for 3–5 minutes.

In the large bowl of an electric mixer, cream the butter with the sugar.

Beat the eggs and add them to the butter mixture, then add the chocolate mixture and blend together.

Resift the flour with the dry ingredients and add to the cake batter alternately with the buttermilk, beating the batter well after each addition. Add the vanilla.

Pour equally into the prepared pans and bake for 25–30 minutes, until a toothpick inserted into the cake comes out clean. When cool, remove from pans.

To make the frosting: In a saucepan, combine the chocolate, sugar, and cream, and cook slowly, stirring, to the soft-ball stage. Cool, add the vanilla, and beat until thick.

Fill the cake with the raspberry jam and frost with the Fudge Frosting.

Serves 8–10.

Dark Chocolate Tube Cake

A rich and opulent cake that looks gorgeous, too.

9-inch or 10-inch tube pan, buttered and dusted with
cocoa

- 2 sticks butter
- 2 cups sugar
- 4 eggs
- 2½ cups cake flour, sifted
- ¼ teaspoon salt
- 1 tablespoon baking soda
- 1 cup sour milk (or 1 cup whole milk with 2 teaspoons fresh lemon juice)
- ¾ cup cocoa
- ⅔ cup boiling water
- 1¼ teaspoons vanilla

Dark and Glossy Frosting:
- 4 tablespoons butter, softened
- ½ cup cocoa
- ¼ teaspoon salt
- 1½ teaspoons vanilla
- 4 cups confectioner's sugar, sifted
- 4–6 tablespoons hot milk

Preheat oven to 350°F.

In the large bowl of an electric mixer, cream together the butter and sugar. Then beat in the eggs, 1 at a time.

Resift the sifted flour with the salt and soda, and add alternately with the sour milk to the butter mixture. Dissolve the cocoa in the boiling water and add to the batter, mixing well. Add the vanilla and beat until all ingredients are well blended. Pour into the prepared tube pan and bake in preheated oven for 1 hour and 10 minutes, until a toothpick inserted into the cake comes out clean. Remove from oven and let cool in pan for 10 minutes. Invert and let cool 5 minutes more, then remove from pan.

To make the frosting: In the small bowl of an electric mixer, blend the butter, cocoa, salt, and vanilla until smooth. Add the confectioner's sugar gradually with the hot milk and beat until smooth and silky.

Frost the cake when cool.

Serves 12.

Chocolate Applesauce Cake

When you "think chocolate," you think chocolate with everything!

---

9 × 9 × 2-inch pan, buttered

     2 cups flour
1½ cups plus 3 tablespoons sugar
     2 teaspoons baking soda
        Pinch salt
     ½ teaspoon nutmeg
     1 teaspoon cinnamon
     ½ teaspoon allspice
     3 tablespoons cocoa plus additional for garnish
     1 cup raisins
     1 cup chopped walnuts
1½ cups unsweetened applesauce
     ½ cup milk
     ½ cup shortening, melted
     1 tablespoon vanilla
     1 cup whipping cream

Preheat oven to 350°F.

Sift together three times the flour, 1½ cups of sugar, baking soda, salt, spices, and cocoa.

Combine the dry ingredients with the raisins and nuts and blend with the applesauce, milk, shortening, and vanilla. Spoon into prepared pan and bake for 45 minutes, until a toothpick inserted into the cake comes out clean. Remove from oven and let cool.

Cut into squares. Whip the cream with the 3 tablespoons of sugar. Serve the squares with a dollop of the sweetened whipped cream, dusted with cocoa.

Serves 8–10.

Chocolate Chip Cake

This is being creative!

---

2 8-inch cake pans, buttered and floured

½ cup vegetable shortening
1½ cups sugar
2½ cups cake flour, sifted
1 tablespoon baking powder
½ teaspoon salt
1 cup milk
1¼ teaspoons vanilla
4 egg whites
½ cup semisweet chocolate bits

Preheat oven to 350°F.

In the large bowl of an electric mixer, cream the shortening with the sugar until light.

Resift the cake flour with baking powder and salt, and add to the sugar mixture alternately with the milk and vanilla, blending well.

On a large platter, beat the egg whites to a peak. Fold in the chocolate bits and fold the whites gently into the cake batter. Spoon equally into prepared pans and bake for 35–40 minutes, until a toothpick inserted into the cake comes out clean. Remove from oven and let cool in pans about 10 minutes, then remove from pans and allow to finish cooling on a rack.

Fill and frost with Easy Chocolate Frosting (p. 42).

Serves 8–10.

Bourbon Street Cake

A fabulous fusion of chocolate and coffee!

---

3 8-inch cake pans, buttered and dusted with cocoa

4½ squares (4½ ounces) bitter chocolate
1 tablespoon instant coffee
½ cup water
1 cup firmly packed dark brown sugar
1 stick butter, softened
1 cup granulated sugar
3 eggs
2½ cups cake flour, sifted
2 teaspoons baking powder
½ teaspoon baking soda
¼ teaspoon salt
1 cup milk
1 tablespoon Kahlua

Preheat oven to 350°F.

In the top of a double boiler over hot but not boiling water, melt the chocolate with the coffee, water, and brown sugar, stirring frequently. Remove from heat and cool.

In the large bowl of an electric mixer, combine the butter with the granulated sugar and beat until light. Add eggs, 1 at a time, beating after each addition, and continue to beat until the batter is well blended. Add the chocolate-sugar mixture and beat until no streaks are left.

Resift the flour with the balance of the dry ingredients and add to the batter alternately with the milk and Kahlua.

Spoon the batter evenly into cake pans and bake in preheated oven for 25–30 minutes, until a toothpick inserted into the cake comes out clean.

Remove from oven and let cool about 10 minutes.

Fill and frost with Mocha Butter Frosting (p. 42).

Serves 8–10.

Chocolate Rum Fruitcake

If you like chocolate, you include it in everything, even fruitcake.

---

9 × 13 × 2-inch pan, buttered and dusted with cocoa

2	cups flour, sifted
1¼	cups sugar
¼	cup cocoa
2	teaspoons baking soda
1	teaspoon cinnamon
½	teaspoon nutmeg
½	teaspoon allspice
	Pinch salt
1½	cups applesauce
½	cup milk
2	tablespoons dark rum
1	cup chopped raisins
1	cup chopped pecans
½	cup chopped pitted dates
¼	cup dark rum

Preheat oven to 350°F.

Into a mixing bowl, resift the flour with all dry ingredients. Add the balance of the ingredients except the ¼ cup of dark rum and blend well.

Spread the batter into the prepared pan and bake for 45 minutes, until the cake springs back when touched lightly. Cool in pan about 10 minutes.

Remove to cake plate and while still warm sprinkle with ¼ cup of dark rum. When completely cold, wrap in foil and store for 24 hours before serving.

Serves 16.

Chocolate Fruitcake

When refrigerated, this cake keeps for a month. It makes a wonderful holiday gift.

---

9 × 5 × 3-inch pan, buttered, lined with buttered wax paper

3 eggs
1 cup sugar
¾ teaspoon vanilla
1½ cups flour
1½ teaspoons baking powder
¼ teaspoon salt
2 cups finely chopped blanched almonds
1 cup diced pitted dates
1 cup diced glacéed cherries
1 cup semisweet chocolate bits
Sliced, toasted almonds
Cherry halves

Preheat oven to 325°F.

In the large bowl of an electric mixer, beat the eggs until frothy and slowly beat in the sugar and vanilla until well blended.

Sift the flour with the baking powder and salt, and add to batter, mixing well.

Fold in the almonds, dates, glacéed cherries, and chocolate, and spoon the batter into the prepared pan. Bake in preheated oven for 1¼–1½ hours, until a toothpick inserted in the cake comes out clean. Cool thoroughly on a rack, remove from pan, and peel off paper. When thoroughly cold, wrap in foil and place in refrigerator.

To serve, decorate with sliced toasted almonds and cherry halves.
Serves 12.

Apricot Upside-Down Cake

What could be better than apricots, coconut, and chocolate!

9-inch square cake pan

½ cup firmly packed dark brown sugar
4 tablespoons butter, melted
  17-ounce can apricot halves, drained; reserve syrup
⅔ cup grated coconut
4 squares (4 ounces) sweet chocolate
1½ cups cake flour, sifted
1 cup plus 3 tablespoons sugar
½ teaspoon baking soda
½ teaspoon baking powder
½ teaspoon salt
5½ tablespoons butter, softened
¾ cup buttermilk
1 teaspoon vanilla
2 eggs
1 cup whipping cream

Preheat oven to 350°F.

Combine the brown sugar with the melted butter and spread over the bottom of the cake pan. Place the apricot halves, cut side down, on top and sprinkle with the 2 tablespoons of reserved syrup and the coconut.

In the top of a double boiler over hot but not boiling water; melt the chocolate, then let cool.

Resift the flour with 1 cup of sugar, the baking soda, baking powder, and salt.

In the large bowl of an electric mixer, put the softened butter and add the flour mixture with ⅓ cup of the buttermilk and vanilla. Beat on medium speed for about 2 minutes. Add the melted chocolate, eggs, and the balance of the buttermilk. Beat 1 minute more and spoon over apricots. Bake in preheated oven for 45–50 minutes, until a toothpick inserted into the cake comes out clean. Remove from oven and cool in pan for 5 minutes, then invert onto plate.

Whip the cream with the 3 tablespoons of sugar.

Serve the cake warm with lightly sweetened whipped cream.

Serves 8.

Cocoa Pound Cake

A welcome departure from the plain pound cake.

10-inch tube pan, buttered

3 cups sugar
3 cups flour
1 cup cocoa
1 tablespoon baking powder
¾ teaspoon salt
2 sticks butter, softened
1½ cups milk
1¼ tablespoons vanilla
3 eggs
¼ cup light cream
  Confectioner's sugar

Preheat oven to 325°F.

In the large bowl of an electric mixer, sift together the dry ingredients.

Add the butter, milk, and vanilla, and beat mixture on medium speed for about 5 minutes, scraping down the sides frequently.

Add eggs, 1 at a time, beating well after each addition. Add cream and continue to beat until mixture is thoroughly blended.

Pour the batter into prepared pan and bake for about 1½ hours, until the cake shrinks from the sides of the pan. Cool cake, then remove from pan.

To serve, dust with sifted confectioner's sugar.

Serves 10–12.

Cocoa Sponge

The whipped cream filling and topping makes this cake deliciously different.

---

2 9-inch pans, lightly buttered and lined with wax paper

6 eggs, separated
1 cup plus 3 tablespoons sugar
6½ tablespoons cocoa
1 teaspoon vanilla
1 teaspoon almond extract
¾ teaspoon cinnamon

Filling and Topping:
1½ cups heavy cream
¼ cup sugar
2 tablespoons cocoa
½ teaspoon vanilla
Semisweet chocolate, grated

Preheat oven to 350°F.

In the large bowl of an electric mixer, beat the egg yolks until thick and fluffy. Add the sugar and continue to beat until smooth, then add cocoa, flavorings, and cinnamon.

On a large open platter, beat the egg whites to stiff peaks, then gently but thoroughly fold them into the batter.

Spoon the batter evenly into the two prepared pans and bake for 25 minutes. Cakes will be done when they pull slightly from the sides of pans.

Remove from oven and cool for 5–6 minutes, then remove from pans and peel off wax paper. Cool cakes completely.

To make the filling: Blend together the heavy cream, sugar, cocoa, and vanilla, and chill for 2 hours. Beat the mixture with an electric beater until thick, and spread between layers and onto top and sides of cake. Decorate with grated semisweet chocolate.

Serves 10.

Company Sponge Roll

Here's an easy but impressive-looking dessert for your guests.

---

10 × 15-inch pan, buttered and floured

5 eggs, separated
1 cup sugar plus additional as needed
5 tablespoons cocoa
¼ cup cake flour, sifted
Pinch salt
1¼ teaspoons vanilla
1 cup whipping cream
Confectioner's sugar
1 tablespoon liqueur
Chopped nuts

Preheat oven to 350°F.

In a bowl, combine the egg yolks with 1 cup of the sugar and beat until light. Add the cocoa sifted with the flour and salt. Stir in the vanilla and mix well.

On a large open platter, beat the egg whites until stiff, then fold gently into the cake batter. Pour evenly into the pan and bake for about 10 minutes, until the cake springs back when lightly touched.

Turn the cake out onto wax paper that has been sprinkled with sugar. Roll up while hot and cover with a damp cloth. Refrigerate, then unroll.

Whip the cream with the confectioner's sugar to taste and your favorite liqueur. Fill the roll with the sweetened whipped cream, reroll, and cover with a chocolate frosting (pp. 42–45). Garnish with chopped nuts.

Serves 8–10.

Passover Sponge Cake

10-inch ungreased tube pan

¼ cup cocoa
¾ cup matzo cake meal
¼ cup potato starch
9 eggs, separated
2 cups sugar
1 tablespoon grated orange zest
¾ cup orange juice
¼ cup water
Confectioner's sugar

Preheat oven to 350°F.

Sift together the cocoa, matzo meal, and potato starch. Set aside. On a large open platter beat the egg whites until foamy. Gradually add the sugar and beat until stiff. Beat in the egg yolks, 1 at a time, and blend well.

Add the orange zest, and then the orange juice and water alternately with the sifted dry ingredients. Fold until all streaks disappear.

Spoon into the tube pan and bake for 55–60 minutes. Invert to cool. Remove from pan and dust with confectioner's sugar.

Serves 10–12.

Easy Whipped Cream Log

Nothing could be easier!

---

10 × 15-inch pan, buttered and floured

5 eggs, separated
½ cup confectioner's sugar, plus additional as needed
2½ tablespoons cocoa
½ teaspoon vanilla
1 pint ice cream, any flavor
   or
1 cup whipping cream
1 tablespoon liqueur

Preheat oven to 350°F.

In the bowl of an electric mixer, combine the yolks and ½ cup of sugar and beat until light and lemony. Add the cocoa to the egg yolks.

On a large open platter, beat the egg whites until stiff. Fold gently into the egg mixture. Add the vanilla. Pour evenly into the pan and bake in preheated oven for 10 minutes. Reduce temperature to 300°F and bake 5 minutes more.

Turn out the cake onto wax paper that has been sprinkled with confectioner's sugar. Roll up while hot and cover with a damp cloth. Refrigerate.

Unroll and fill with softened ice cream. Or whip the cream with 3 tablespoons of confectioner's sugar and your favorite liqueur, and fill. In either case, reroll and serve.

Serves 8–10.

Chocolate Spice Roll

Cookie sheet, buttered and lined with buttered wax paper

 4 eggs
 ¼ teaspoon salt
 ¾ teaspoon baking powder
 ¾ cup sugar
 ¼ teaspoon cinnamon
 1 teaspoon vanilla
 ¾ cup cake flour, sifted
    Confectioner's sugar

Icing:

12 ounces semisweet chocolate bits
 4 tablespoons butter
 ⅔ cup sifted confectioner's sugar plus additional as needed
 ¾ teaspoon cinnamon
 ¼ cup evaporated milk
 1 teaspoon vanilla
    Pinch salt

Preheat oven to 400°F.

In the top of a double boiler over hot but not boiling water, beat the eggs with the salt and baking powder until frothy. Combine sugar and cinnamon and beat into the egg mixture. Beat until thick. Remove from heat and add the vanilla and sifted flour. Pour the batter into the prepared cookie sheet and bake in preheated oven for about 10–12 minutes. It is done when springy to the touch.

Turn out on a cloth or paper dusted with confectioner's sugar. Remove the buttered paper, trim off crisp edges with a sharp knife, and roll up in the paper, jelly-roll fashion. Cool.

To make the icing: In a double boiler over hot but not boiling water, melt the chocolate and butter. Remove from heat and stir in the sugar, cinnamon, milk, vanilla, and salt. Beat until smooth.

Unroll cake and frost inside of roll. Roll up and frost outside, then dust with confectioner's sugar.

Serves 8–10.

Chocolate Roll with Preserves

Cookie sheet, buttered and floured

4 eggs, separated
¾ cup sugar
2 tablespoons butter or shortening
1 cup cake flour, sifted
2½ tablespoons cocoa
   Pinch salt
2 teaspoons baking powder
¼ cup cold water
¼ teaspoon vanilla
1 cup apricot or raspberry preserves
   Confectioner's sugar

Preheat oven to 375°F.

Combine the egg yolks, sugar, and butter and beat until light and lemony.

Resift the flour with the cocoa and salt and baking powder. Add to the egg mixture alternately with the water. Add the vanilla.

On a large open platter, beat the egg whites with the salt until stiff. Fold gently into the batter. Bake in preheated oven for 10–12 minutes, until cake springs back when lightly touched. Remove from pan to wax paper, remove crisp edges, and roll. Wrap in wax paper until cool. Unroll and fill with preserves. Reroll and dust with confectioner's sugar or ice with chocolate frosting (pp. 42–45).

Serves 8–10.

Rum Raisin Icebox Cake

The combination of dark rum, raisins, and chocolate leads me to believe this cake is Spanish in origin.

8-inch cake pan, buttered and lined with foil

- ¾ cup raisins
- ¾ cup boiling water
- 4 tablespoons dark rum
- 4½ ounces bitter chocolate, broken into pieces
- ¼ cup evaporated milk
- 1 stick butter
- 10 tablespoons extra-fine sugar
- 2 eggs, separated
- 1¼ cups vanilla cookie crumbs
- ½ teaspoon vanilla
- 1 cup heavy cream
- 3 tablespoons sugar

Bitter chocolate, grated

Soak the raisins in boiling water for about 10 minutes. Drain, reserving 3 tablespoons of the water, then cover the raisins with 2 tablespoons of the rum.

In the top of a double boiler over simmering water, combine the chocolate pieces with milk and raisin water until melted. Cool.

Beat the butter with 5 tablespoons of the extra-fine sugar until fluffy. Add the egg yolks, 1 at a time, the melted chocolate, crumbs, vanilla, and raisins with the rum.

On a large open platter, beat the egg whites until stiff, gradually adding the remaining 5 tablespoons of extra-fine sugar. Fold into the chocolate mixture gently but thoroughly.

Spoon the mixture into the prepared cake pan and chill overnight. Invert the cake onto a serving plate, removing the foil.

Whip the cream with the sugar and the remaining rum.

To serve, garnish with the sweetened whipped cream and top with grated bitter chocolate.

Serves 10.

Chocolate Delmonico Cake

A spectacular finish to any dinner.

8-inch cake pan, buttered

No. 2½ can fruit cocktail
14½-ounce can evaporated milk
4 eggs, beaten
⅓ cup plus 3 tablespoons sugar
1 teaspoon grated lemon rind
1½ teaspoons vanilla
9-inch chocolate layer cake, split into 2 layers
(Semisweet Chocolate Cake [p. 18] *or* Peggy's
Chocolate Cake [p. 20])
1 cup whipping cream

Preheat oven to 325°F.

Drain the fruit and reserve ¾ of the syrup. Put the fruit aside.

In a small saucepan, combine the ¾ cup of syrup with the evaporated milk; scald. Mix the beaten eggs with ⅓ cup of the sugar. Very gradually stir the eggs into the milk mixture. Add lemon rind, 1 teaspoon of vanilla, and 1 cup of the reserved fruit cocktail. Pour into prepared pan set in a pan of hot water, and bake in preheated oven for 30–35 minutes, or until knife inserted in custard comes out clean. Remove from the water and let cool.

Place 1 cake layer over custard, invert on platter to turn out, and top with other layer. Chill.

Whip the cream and add 3 tablespoons of the sugar and ½ teaspoon of vanilla. Frost the cake and garnish with the remaining fruit cocktail. Chill.

Serves 6–8.

Filled Chocolate Angel Food Cake

This is always a welcome dessert.

10-inch tube pan, *not* buttered

12 egg whites
 1 teaspoon cream of tartar
 1 teaspoon vanilla
 ¾ cup flour, sifted
 2 cups extra-fine sugar
 ½ cup plus 3 tablespoons cocoa
 2 cups whipping cream
 ¾ cup confectioner's sugar
 1 teaspoon vanilla
   Slivered toasted almonds (optional)

Preheat oven to 400°F.

On a large open platter, beat the egg whites until foamy, add cream of tartar, and continue beating until stiff.

Sift the flour, extra-fine sugar, and ½ cup of cocoa together, and gradually fold into the egg whites and vanilla.

Bake in dry tube pan in preheated oven for 40 minutes, until cake pulls from sides. Invert to cool.

Whip the cream and add the 3 tablespoons of cocoa, confectioner's sugar, and vanilla. Chill several hours to set flavors. Split cake in 2 layers and fill and cover cake with whipped cream or Chocolate Custard Filling (p. 44). Garnish with slivered toasted almonds, if desired.

Serves 10–12.

Sweet Chocolate Muffins

Perfect for a tea table. And this recipe can be doubled.

Muffin tin, 8 paper baking cups

1 egg, separated
¾ cup sugar
2 tablespoons butter, melted
1½ squares (1½ ounces) bitter chocolate, melted
1 cup cake flour
1 teaspoon baking powder
¼ teaspoon salt
⅔ cup milk
1¼ teaspoon vanilla
Confectioner's sugar for garnish

Preheat oven to 375°F.

Beat the egg yolk with the sugar until thick and lemony. Add the butter and chocolate, and blend well.

Sift the dry ingredients together and add alternately to the chocolate mixture with the milk and vanilla.

On a large open platter, beat the egg white until stiff and fold gently into the batter.

Spoon the batter into baking cups placed in a muffin tin and bake in preheated oven for 15 minutes, until tops spring back when lightly touched.

When cool, dust with confectioner's sugar for garnish.

Serves 8.

Cupcakes for Your Lovable Little Ones

A recipe for a 2-layer 8-inch cake will make about 24 medium cupcakes. A recipe for a 2-layer 9-inch cake will make about 30 medium cupcakes. They can be baked in buttered muffin tins or fluted cupcake papers. Preheat oven to 375°F. and bake for 15–20 minutes, until tops spring back when lightly touched. Top with your favorite frosting when cool, or see Frostings and Fillings chapter (pp. 42–45) for some new ideas.

FROSTINGS AND FILLINGS

Easy Chocolate Frosting
Mocha Butter Frosting
Chocolate Maple Frosting
Crème Ganache
Chocolate Custard Filling
Chocolate Spice Spread
Cocoa Cinnamon Muffin Topper
Practically Obscene Chocolate
Chestnut Filling and Topping
Chocolate Glaze

Easy Chocolate Frosting

If the frosting is too thick, beat in just a little cream. If the frosting is too thin, beat in a little more confectioner's sugar.

---

    3 cups sugar
    1 cup water
    2 tablespoons light corn syrup
    2 tablespoons butter
    4 squares (4 ounces) bittersweet chocolate
 1½ teaspoons vanilla

In a saucepan over low heat, combine all ingredients except vanilla, stirring until ingredients are mixed well. Cover and bring to a boil. Then quickly uncover and cook without stirring until the temperature on a candy thermometer reaches 234°F.—soft-ball stage. Remove from heat and cool. Add vanilla and beat with rotary beater until thick enough to spread.

Makes 3½ cups.

Mocha Butter Frosting

---

    1 stick butter, softened
    2 cups sifted confectioner's sugar
    1 tablespoon cocoa
  ⅛ teaspoon salt
  ¼ cup extra-strong coffee
    1 tablespoon Kahlua

In an electric mixer, combine the butter with the sugar, cocoa, and salt, and beat until creamy. Add the coffee and Kahlua, and continue beating until the frosting is creamy and spreadable.

Fill and frost the cake, and chill before serving.

Makes 2½ cups.

Chocolate Maple Frosting

This frosting will charm any Vermonter into the kitchen to bake a chocolate cake, for that is what this frosting and filling should grace.

---

  2 egg whites
½ cup pure maple syrup
  4 tablespoons water
⅛ teaspoon salt
  2 squares (2 ounces) bitter chocolate, melted

In the top of a double boiler over rapidly boiling water, combine the egg whites, syrup, water, and salt, and cook for 7 minutes, beating constantly. Remove from heat, add melted chocolate, and continue beating until mixture stands in stiff peaks. Delish!

Enough for a 3-layer 8-inch cake.

Crème Ganache

This is probably the most divine filling or frosting ever devised. Everyone should learn to make it.

---

  4 squares (4 ounces) semisweet chocolate
  2 tablespoons butter, softened
½ cup heavy cream, whipped

In the top of a double boiler over hot but not boiling water, melt the chocolate. Remove from heat and stir in the softened butter. Cool thoroughly, then fold in the whipped cream.

Makes 1½ cups.

Chocolate Custard Filling

½ cup plus 2 tablespoons sugar
5 tablespoons flour
¼ teaspoon salt
2 cups milk, scalded
2 eggs, beaten lightly
2 ounces bitter chocolate
1 teaspoon vanilla
1 tablespoon brandy

Combine the sugar, the flour, and the salt in top of a double boiler. Add the scalded milk and blend until smooth; then add the beaten eggs. Place the custard over hot water, add the chocolate, and cook, stirring until blended and thickened. Remove from heat and add the vanilla and the brandy.

Sufficient for 3 8-inch or 9-inch cake layers.

Chocolate Spice Spread

Chocolate for breakfast or for snacks.

½ cup cocoa
5 tablespoons butter, melted
1 teaspoon cinnamon
6 tablespoons sugar

Combine all ingredients and blend well. Spread on hot, crisp toast or toasted English muffins, or refrigerate to keep.

Enough for 4–6 people.

Cocoa Cinnamon Muffin Topper

Different and good with hot coffee.

2½ tablespoons butter
¼ cup cocoa
½ teaspoon cinnamon
3 tablespoons sugar

Melt the butter and blend with the other ingredients.
Spread on hot toasted English muffins.
Makes enough for 4.

Practically Obscene Chocolate Chestnut Filling and Topping

Expensive but worth it. I prefer it with a chocolate cake.

---

2 sticks plus 3 tablespoons butter
1 cup extra-fine sugar
1 egg
5 tablespoons dark rum
1 teaspoon vanilla
3 squares (3 ounces) semisweet chocolate, melted
1 1-pound can chestnut puree
Semisweet chocolate, grated (optional)

In the large bowl of an electric mixer, combine all but the chocolate and chestnut puree and beat until the mixture is light and fluffy. Add the melted chocolate and puree, and blend thoroughly.

Chill the mixture until it is firm enough to spread as filling and frosting. After frosting, garnish with grated semisweet chocolate, if desired.

Sufficient to fill and frost a 10-inch layer cake.

Chocolate Glaze

1 square (1 ounce) bitter chocolate
3 squares (3 ounces) dark sweet chocolate
¼ cup water
4 tablespoons butter
4 tablespoons confectioner's sugar
1 teaspoon honey

In the top of a double boiler over hot water, melt the chocolates in the water. Remove from heat and add the butter, sugar, and honey. Blend well and spoon over top and sides of torte.

Makes enough for one 9-inch torte.

TORTES

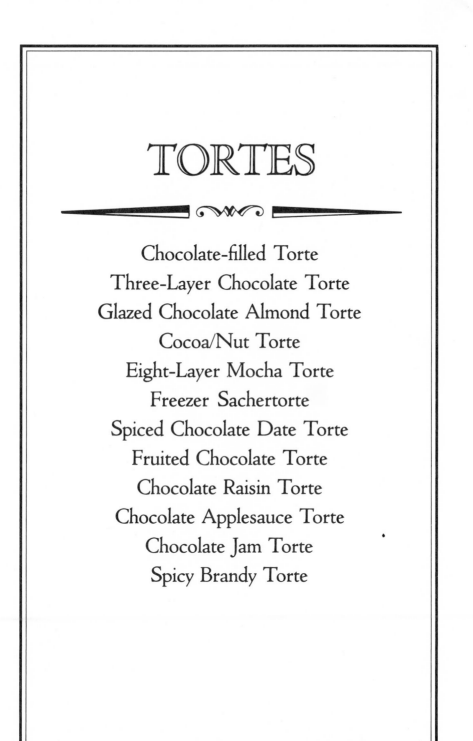

Chocolate-filled Torte
Three-Layer Chocolate Torte
Glazed Chocolate Almond Torte
Cocoa/Nut Torte
Eight-Layer Mocha Torte
Freezer Sachertorte
Spiced Chocolate Date Torte
Fruited Chocolate Torte
Chocolate Raisin Torte
Chocolate Applesauce Torte
Chocolate Jam Torte
Spicy Brandy Torte

Three-Layer Chocolate Torte

You can fill this with Chocolate Custard (p. 44) or your favorite jelly. Then top with more chocolate (Frostings, pp. 42–45) or sweetened whipped cream.

---

 3 8-inch cake pans, buttered

10 eggs, separated
 1 cup sugar
 1 cup ground almonds
 1 cup grated dark sweet chocolate
 1 tablespoon brandy or wine
 1 cup dry bread crumbs
 ½ teaspoon cinnamon
 ½ teaspoon ground cloves
 1 teaspoon baking powder
   Juice of one lemon
   Grated rind of one lemon
 ¼ teaspoon vanilla
   Pinch salt
   Chocolate Custard Filling (p. 44)
   or
 1 cup raspberry or apricot jelly

Preheat oven to 350°F.

In the large bowl of an electric mixer, combine the yolks and sugar, and beat until light. Add the nuts and chocolate; beat again. Add the next 8 ingredients. Beat well.

On a large open platter, beat the whites with the pinch of salt until stiff. Fold gently into the torte mixture. Pour equally into the prepared pans and bake in preheated oven for about 20 minutes, until the top appears dry. Cool.

When completely cool, fill with Chocolate Custard Filling (p. 44) and ice with a chocolate icing. *Or* fill with jelly and cover with chocolate frosting (pp. 42–45) or sweetened whipped cream.

Serves 8–10.

Chocolate-filled Torte

Tortes are very easy to make. As a rule they contain no butter and substitute ground nuts and/or bread crumbs for flour.

---

2 9-inch cake pans, buttered

4 squares (4 ounces) bitter chocolate
1 cup milk
5 eggs, separated
2 cups sugar
1 cup flour
1 teaspoon baking powder
  Pinch salt

Filling and Frosting:
5 squares (5 ounces) Maillard's semisweet chocolate, if
   available
3 tablespoons sugar
  Pinch salt
3 tablespoons water
3 egg yolks, beaten
1½ cups whipping cream

Preheat oven to 325°F.

In a small saucepan over very low heat, melt the chocolate in the milk. Cool. Cream together the yolks and the sugar. Blend in the dry ingredients and the chocolate mixture.

On a large open platter, beat the egg whites until stiff. Fold the egg whites gently into the batter. Pour the batter equally into the prepared pans and bake in preheated oven for about 25 minutes, until the top of the torte springs back when lightly touched. Cool.

To make the filling: In the top of a double boiler over hot but not boiling water, combine the chocolate, sugar, salt, and water, and cook until smooth and thick. Remove from heat, cool slightly, and very gradually add the beaten egg yolks, stirring constantly. Cool.

Whip the cream and fold in. Fill and frost the cake.
Serves 10–12.

Glazed Chocolate Almond Torte

I believe in the sound advice: Everything in moderation—except chocolate!

9-inch springform, lightly buttered, lined with wax paper, and lightly buttered again

- 12 tablespoons fine dry bread crumbs
- 4½ squares (4½ ounces) semisweet chocolate
- 1¾ cups blanched almonds
- 1 tablespoon baking powder
- 1 stick butter
- 1 cup sugar
- 6 eggs, separated
- 2½ tablespoons Kirschwasser

Glaze:
- 1 square (1 ounce) bitter chocolate
- 3 squares (3 ounces) dark sweet chocolate
- ¼ cup water
- 4 tablespoons butter
- 4 tablespoons confectioner's sugar
- 1 teaspoon honey

Preheat oven to 350°F.

Sprinkle the bottom and sides of the prepared springform with 6 tablespoons of the bread crumbs. Combine the chocolate and almonds in a blender and grate. Remove from the blender and add 6 tablespoons of bread crumbs and the baking powder.

In an electric mixer, cream together the butter and sugar, and beat until fluffy. Add the egg yolks and beat on high speed until well blended.

Remove the beaters and stir in the nut mixture with the liqueur.

On a large open platter, beat the egg whites until they peak, then fold them gently into the torte mixture.

Spoon the batter into the prepared springform and bake in

preheated oven for 1 hour, until the top of the torte springs back when lightly touched. Remove from oven and cool.

To make the glaze: In the top of a double boiler over hot water, melt the chocolate in the water. Remove from heat and add the butter, sugar, and honey. Blend well and spoon over top and sides of torte.
Serves 10.

Cocoa/Nut Torte

This is good served hot or cold.

9-inch glass baking dish

  2 tablespoons bread crumbs
1¼ cups ground walnuts
  ¾ cup sugar
  ⅓ cup cocoa
  4 eggs, separated
  1 teaspoon vanilla
  1 teaspoon grated lemon rind

Preheat oven to 350°F.

Dust the buttered baking dish with the bread crumbs.

Combine the walnuts, sugar, and cocoa in a bowl. Beat the egg yolks, then gradually add to the nut mixture, beating well. Add the vanilla and grated lemon rind, and mix well.

On a large open platter, beat the egg whites until stiff and fold them gently into the mixture. Pour the mixture into the prepared baking dish and bake in preheated oven for 30 minutes, until the top of the torte springs back when lightly touched.
Serves 6–8.

Eight-Layer Mocha Torte

The layers are easier to split if you freeze them first.

Jelly-roll pan, buttered, lined with wax paper, buttered again

- ¾ cup cake flour, sifted
- ½ teaspoon baking powder
- ½ teaspoon salt
- 2½ squares (2½ ounces) bitter chocolate
- 5 eggs
- ¾ cup plus 2 tablespoons sugar
- ¼ cup cold water
- ¼ teaspoon baking soda

Icing:
- 2 tablespoons instant coffee
- 2 tablespoons hot milk
- ⅔ cup butter
- 1 pound confectioner's sugar, sifted
- 2 egg whites
- 1 teaspoon vanilla

Glaze:
- 1 square (1 ounce) bitter chocolate
- 1 tablespoon butter
- 1½ tablespoons hot milk
- ½ cup confectioner's sugar, sifted
- Pinch salt

Preheat oven to 350°F.

To the flour add the baking powder and salt and sift again.

In the top of a double boiler over hot but not boiling water, melt the chocolate.

Beat the eggs until light and add the ¾ cup of sugar slowly, beating constantly. Blend in the flour mixture.

Remove the chocolate from heat and quickly add the cold water, baking soda, and 2 tablespoons of sugar. Stir until thick and smooth, then stir into the cake batter. Pour into the jelly-roll pan and bake in preheated oven for 18–20 minutes, until the top springs back when lightly touched. When done, turn out on a towel sprinkled with confectioner's sugar. Remove wax paper, trim off crisp edges, and cool. Cut cake into four equal parts and chill thoroughly, then split each layer, making eight layers.

To make the icing: Dissolve the coffee in the hot milk. Cool.

Cream the butter, add 1 cup of the confectioner's sugar, and cream well. Add the dissolved coffee to the butter and mix well. Add the remaining confectioner's sugar, egg whites, and vanilla, and blend. Beat over ice until the right consistency to spread. Frost one layer, put another layer on top. Continue frosting to last layer. Chill the frosted cake.

To make the glaze: In the top of a double boiler over hot but not boiling water, melt the chocolate and butter together.

In a bowl, combine the milk, confectioner's sugar, and salt. Add the melted chocolate mixture gradually, stirring well. While glaze is still warm, spread it with a knife over the chilled torte, allowing it to drip over the sides.

Serves 12.

Freezer Sachertorte

This cake freezes well and so may be made ahead of time.

8-inch springform pan, buttered and floured

⅓ cup soft butter
6 tablespoons sugar
3 squares (3 ounces) semisweet chocolate, melted
4 egg yolks
½ cup plus 1 tablespoon flour, sifted
5 egg whites
5 tablespoons apricot jam

Frosting:
½ cup sugar
⅓ cup water
3½ squares (3½ ounces) semisweet chocolate

Preheat oven to 325°F.

Cream the butter, add the sugar gradually, and beat until light. Add the melted chocolate and mix well. Add egg yolks, 1 at a time, blending well, and add the sifted flour.

On a large open platter, beat the egg whites until stiff but not dry. Fold them into the batter.

Turn the batter into the prepared pan and bake on lower shelf of the oven for 1 hour and 15 minutes, until the top of the cake springs back when lightly touched. Let the cake stand 10 minutes on a rack before removing springform. Release form and cool completely.

Split the cake in half, spread with half of the apricot jam for filling, top with the other half of the cake, and cover with the rest of the jam.

To make the frosting: In a saucepan, combine the sugar and water, and simmer, stirring, for 2 minutes. Remove from heat. Add the chocolate and stir until melted and smooth. Bring to a boil, stirring. Remove from heat and stir until the mixture starts to thicken. Pour over the cake—top and sides. If frozen, thaw cake at least 1 hour before serving.

Serves 8–10.

Spiced Chocolate Date Torte

9-inch springform pan, buttered

         9 eggs
1¾ cups plus 3 tablespoons sugar
         1 cup finely chopped pitted dates
         4 tablespoons lemon juice
         3 tablespoons ground almonds
1½ tablespoons shredded citron
     ¼ cup grated dark sweet chocolate
     ¾ teaspoon cinnamon
     ¾ teaspoon allspice
1¼ cup graham cracker crumbs
     ½ teaspoon baking powder
         Pinch salt
         1 cup whipping cream

Preheat oven to 350°F.

Separate 7 of the eggs.

Beat the 2 whole eggs with the 7 yolks until light and lemony. Add 1¾ cups of the sugar and beat again. Add the dates, lemon juice, almonds, and citron. Blend well.

Add the chocolate, cinnamon, allspice, crumbs, and baking powder, and beat until smooth.

On a large open platter, beat the egg whites with the salt until stiff but not dry. Fold the egg whites into the batter and pour into the prepared springform. Bake for 40–60 minutes, until the top springs back when lightly touched. Cool 10 minutes before removing form.

Whip the cream with the remaining 3 tablespoons of sugar and serve with the cooled cake.

Serves 10–12.

Fruited Chocolate Torte

8-inch square pan, buttered

2 eggs
½ cup flour
Pinch salt
1 teaspoon baking powder
2 tablespoons cocoa
½ cup sugar
½ teaspoon vanilla
1 cup chopped pecans or walnuts
2 cups chopped pitted dates
⅛ cup chopped candied cherries

Preheat oven to 350°F.

Beat the eggs until light.

Sift together all the dry ingredients and blend into the eggs.

Add the rest of the ingredients, mix, and pour into the prepared pan.

Bake in preheated oven for 1 hour, until the top appears dry. Allow to cool before cutting.

Serves 6–8.

Chocolate Raisin Torte

8-inch springform, buttered

4 eggs, separated
½ cup plus 3 tablespoons sugar
⅓ cup ground almonds
⅓ cup raisins
⅓ cup matzo cake flour, sifted
¼ cup sweet red wine
⅓ cup orange juice
4 squares (4 ounces) dark sweet chocolate, grated
Pinch salt
1 cup whipping cream
or
confectioner's sugar

Preheat oven to 350°F.

Combine the yolks and the sugar, and beat until very light. Add the ground nuts, raisins, matzo meal, wine, and orange juice. Blend well and add the chocolate.

On a large open platter, beat the egg whites with a pinch of salt until stiff, then gently fold into the batter. Pour into the prepared springform and bake in the preheated oven for 1 hour, until the top springs back when touched lightly. Cool completely.

To serve, either whip the cream with 3 tablespoons of sugar as a garnish, or dust with confectioner's sugar.

Serves 6–8.

Chocolate Applesauce Torte

3 8-inch cake pans, buttered

6 eggs, separated
1 cup sugar
3 tablespoons cocoa
½ cup applesauce
¼ teaspoon vanilla
1 cup graham cracker crumbs or bread crumbs
1½ teaspoons baking powder
   Pinch salt
1½ cups of your favorite chocolate butter frosting

Preheat oven to 350°F.

Beat the yolks with the sugar until light. Mix in the cocoa, applesauce, and vanilla.

Combine the crumbs with the baking powder and add to the batter.

On a large open platter, beat the egg whites with the pinch of salt until stiff but not dry. Fold gently into the batter. Pour equally into prepared pans and bake in preheated oven for about 20 minutes, until top springs back when lightly touched. Cool.

Frost and fill with your choice of chocolate frosting.

Serves 8–10.

Chocolate Jam Torte

2 8-inch cake pans, buttered

1 cup sugar

6 eggs, separated

¾ cup vanilla, graham cracker, or zweiback crumbs

1 teaspoon baking powder

1 cup grated dark sweet chocolate

¾ cup ground almonds

¾ teaspoon ground cloves

¾ teaspoon cinnamon

¼ teaspoon vanilla

Pinch salt

½ cup jam or jelly

½ cup raspberry jam

or

½ cup chocolate frosting

Preheat oven to 325°F.

Beat the sugar and egg yolks until very light.

Combine the crumbs with the baking powder. Blend together the grated chocolate, ground almonds, ground cloves, cinnamon, and vanilla. Mix until well blended.

On a large open platter, beat the egg whites with the pinch of salt until stiff. Fold gently into the torte mixture. Pour into the prepared cake pans and bake in preheated oven for 20–25 minutes, until the top springs back when lightly touched.

Cool and fill with raspberry jam or jelly, then top with raspberry jam or your favorite chocolate frosting.

Serves 8–10.

Spicy Brandy Torte

Top this with your favorite chocolate frosting or glaze.

10-inch springform pan; do *not* butter

- 10 eggs, separated
- 2 cups sugar
- 1¾ cups fine rye bread crumbs
- ¾ cup ground almonds
- ¼ cup chopped citron
- 1 bar (4 ounces) German sweet chocolate, grated
  Grated rind of 1 orange
  Grated rind of 1 lemon
- 1 tablespoon cinnamon
- 1 teaspoon allspice
- ½ teaspoon ground cloves
- 3 tablespoons brandy
  Pinch salt
- ¾ cup chocolate icing

Preheat oven to 350°F.

Combine the yolks with the sugar and beat until thick and lemony. Add the rest of the ingredients except the egg whites, salt, and icing, and mix well.

On a large open platter, beat the egg whites with the pinch of salt until stiff but not dry. Fold into the batter gently and pour into the springform pan. Bake in preheated oven for 45–60 minutes, until the top springs back when touched lightly. Cool 10 minutes before removing springform.

When cool, frost with your favorite topping.

Serves 12–14.

PIES

Chocolate Coconut Pie Shell
Chocolate Crumb Crust
Brown Derby Black Bottom Pie
Black Bottom Rum Pie
Crème de Cacao Fudge Pie
Chocolate Brandy Pie
Chocolate Chess Pie
Simply Deluscious Pie
Chocolate Cream Pie
Mocha Parfait Pie
Mocha-Choc Chiffon Pie
Velvet Chiffon Pie
Gingered Rum Chocolate Pie
Fresh Strawberry Pie
Chocolate Cherry Pie
Mocha Chocolate Walnut Pie
Fresh Raspberry Pie

Chocolate Coconut Pie Shell

A change of pace for the custard, coconut, or chocolate pie.

9-inch pie plate, buttered

1½ cups flour
 3 tablespoons confectioner's sugar
 4 tablespoons cocoa or 4 tablespoons grated semisweet
     chocolate
 ½ teaspoon salt
 ½ cup shortening
 3 tablespoons ice water
 ⅓ cup flaked coconut

Preheat oven to 450°F.

Sift together the flour, confectioner's sugar, cocoa, and salt.

Cut the shortening into the mixture with a pastry blender until the mixture looks like coarse meal. Add the water, 1 tablespoon at a time, then the flaked coconut.

Gather the dough into a ball, wrap in wax paper, and chill for at least 1 hour.

Roll out on lightly floured board to ⅛ inch thick.

Bake shell in preheated oven for 10 minutes.

Chocolate Crumb Crust

9-inch pie plate, buttered

12 chocolate cookies, crushed
 ½ cup sugar
 6 tablespoons butter, melted

Combine the crushed cookies with the sugar and melted butter. Pat onto the bottom and sides of the pie plate. Chill. Use your favorite filling or ice cream. For ice cream combinations see pp. 163–172.

Brown Derby Black Bottom Pie

The grated orange zest is the "snapper" in this dessert.

9-inch baked pastry shell

1 envelope unflavored gelatin
¾ cup plus additional sugar as needed
⅛ teaspoon salt
1 egg yolk
¾ cup milk
3 squares (3 ounces) bitter chocolate
1 cup evaporated milk
1 teaspoon vanilla
1 cup whipping cream
¼ cup grated orange zest
1 square (1 ounce) bitter chocolate, grated

In the top of a double boiler over hot but not boiling water, combine the gelatin, sugar, salt, egg yolk, milk, and 3 squares of chocolate. Cook, stirring constantly, until the chocolate is melted. Remove from heat and beat with egg beater until smooth. Chill.

Whip the evaporated milk by placing in a freezer tray for about 30 minutes, until crystals form around the edges, then pour into a chilled bowl and whip rapidly until thickened.

Fold in chocolate mixture and vanilla. Pile into the pie shell and chill.

Whip the cream with the sugar to taste. Blend the orange zest into the whipped cream and spread over the top of the pie. Garnish with the grated bitter chocolate.

Serves 8.

Black Bottom Rum Pie

9-inch pie plate, buttered, if making crust

Crust:

1½ cups crushed chocolate cookies
or
gingersnaps
2 tablespoons butter, melted
2 tablespoons confectioner's sugar
or
use a 9-inch pastry shell

Filling:

1 tablespoon unflavored gelatin
¼ cup cold water
2 cups milk
¾ cup sugar
4 teaspoons cornstarch
4 eggs, separated
2 squares (2 ounces) bitter chocolate, melted
¾ teaspoon vanilla
3 tablespoons rum
¼ teaspoon salt
¼ teaspoon cream of tartar

Topping:

1 cup whipping cream
2 tablespoons confectioner's sugar
1 teaspoon rum (optional)
Bitter chocolate, grated

If making the crust, preheat the oven to 325°F.

Blend together the crumbs, butter, and sugar. Pat into prepared pie plate. Bake for 10 minutes or use as is.

To make the filling: Soften the gelatin in the cold water until dissolved.

Scald the milk and set aside.

Mix ½ cup of the sugar with the cornstarch and set aside.

Beat the egg yolks until light and lemony; to them slowly add the milk and then the sugar and cornstarch mixture. Cook in the top of a double boiler over hot but not boiling water, stirring frequently, about 15 minutes. When the custard is thickened, remove 1 cup of custard and add to it the melted chocolate. Blend well and add vanilla. Set aside.

Pour the dissolved gelatin into the remaining custard, which is still hot, and mix well. Cool, then add the rum. Set aside.

Pour the chocolate custard into the pie shell.

On a large open platter, beat the egg whites with the salt and cream of tartar, adding the remaining ¼ cup of sugar gradually. When stiff but not dry, fold the egg whites into the rum custard and spoon over the chocolate layer. Chill well.

To make the topping: Whip the cream with the confectioner's sugar and rum, if you wish. Spread on top of the chilled pie. Top with grated bitter chocolate.

Serves 8–10.

Crème de Cacao Fudge Pie

This is for the happy chocolate lover.

9-inch pie plate, buttered

3 egg whites
⅛ teaspoon salt
½ cup sugar
½ cup crème de cacao
1 cup chocolate cookie crumbs
½ cup chopped walnuts
1 cup whipping cream, whipped
  Semisweet chocolate, coarsely grated

Preheat oven to 325°F.

On a large open platter, beat the egg whites and salt to soft peaks, then slowly add the sugar 1 tablespoon at a time, beating until stiff. Blend in ¼ cup of the liqueur, the crumbs, and walnuts. Spread in prepared pie pan and bake in preheated oven for 30 minutes.

Do not allow to burn.

Remove from oven and cool completely.

Blend the remaining liqueur into the whipped cream. Cover the pie with large dollops of cream and garnish with grated chocolate.

Serves 6–8.

Chocolate Brandy Pie

Brandy with crème de cacao creates a distinctively different dessert.

9-inch pie plate, buttered

Crust:

1½ cups chocolate cookie crumbs
4 tablespoons butter, melted
¼ cup sugar

Filling:

1¾ teaspoons gelatin
⅓ cup heavy cream
4 egg yolks
¼ cup sugar
⅓ cup brandy
⅓ cup crème de cacao
1 cup whipping cream, whipped

Topping:

1 cup whipping cream
2 tablespoons confectioner's sugar
Semisweet chocolate, grated

Preheat oven to 400°F.

Blend together well the cookie crumbs, butter, and sugar. Press onto bottom and sides of pan. Bake for 5 minutes. Cool.

To make the filling: In the top of a double boiler over hot but not boiling water, mix the gelatin with the heavy cream, stirring until dissolved. Remove from heat and cool. Before the gelatin sets, beat the egg yolks until fluffy, gradually adding the sugar. Continue to beat until slightly thickened. Add the brandy and crème de cacao, then the gelatin mixture, and blend. Fold in the whipped cream, spoon into prepared pie shell, and freeze.

To make the topping: Whip the cream with the confectioner's sugar. Remove the pie from the freezer. Garnish with whipped cream and grated semisweet chocolate.

Serves 8.

Chocolate Chess Pie

A welcome departure from the well-known chess pie.

9-inch pie plate, buttered

Pâte Brisée Crust:
1 cup flour, sifted
½ teaspoon sugar
1 stick cold butter
2 tablespoons ice water
Rice

Filling:
1 stick butter
1½ squares (1½ ounces) bitter chocolate
1 cup packed light brown sugar
½ cup granulated sugar
1 tablespoon flour
2 eggs
2 tablespoons milk
1 teaspoon vanilla

Preheat oven to 400°F.

Combine flour and sugar in a chilled bowl. Using a pastry blender or two knives, cut in the cold butter as quickly as possible. When the mixture is pebbly, moisten it little by little with the ice water. When the dough adheres, roll to ⅛ inch thick, fit into pie plate, prick the bottom, and chill for one hour.

Line the pie shell with wax paper, fill with rice, and bake in preheated oven for 10 minutes. Remove the rice and paper from the pie shell and continue to bake shell for 8–10 minutes more. Cool.

Reduce oven to 325°F.

To make the filling: In a saucepan, melt the butter and chocolate over moderate heat. Remove from heat and add the sugars combined with flour. Mix well. Beat in the eggs, milk, and vanilla. Pour into prepared shell and bake for 35–40 minutes, until set. Serve at room temperature.

Serves 8.

Simply Deluscious Pie

A quick and easy delightful dessert.

9-inch pie plate, buttered

Crust:

12 chocolate cookies, crushed

½ cup sugar

6 tablespoons butter, melted

Filling:

1 cup milk

10 large marshmallows

3 ounces curaçao

3 ounces crème de cacao

⅓ cup grated semisweet chocolate

1 cup whipping cream, whipped

Topping:

1 cup whipping cream

2 tablespoons confectioner's sugar

Semisweet chocolate, grated

Combine the crushed cookies with the sugar and melted butter and pat onto the bottom and sides of the pie plate. Chill.

To make the filling: In the top of a double boiler over hot water, heat the milk, add the marshmallows, and stir until melted. Remove from heat and add liqueurs. Cool.

Blend the grated chocolate into the whipped cream and fold into the marshmallow mixture. Spoon into the chilled shell and chill thoroughly.

To make the topping: Whip the cream with the sugar. Top the pie with the sweetened whipped cream and dust the top with grated semisweet chocolate.

Serves 8.

Chocolate Cream Pie

There is no limit to the craving for chocolate!

9-inch pie plate, buttered

Chocolate Pie Shell:

1½ cups flour
½ teaspoon salt
3 tablespoons cocoa
3 tablespoons confectioner's sugar
½ cup shortening
3 tablespoons ice water

Inside Stuff:

4 eggs
⅔ cup sugar
½ teaspoon salt
½ teaspoon nutmeg
2⅔ cups milk
1 teaspoon vanilla

Finishing Touch:

1 square (1 ounce) bitter chocolate
2 tablespoons butter
½ cup confectioner's sugar, sifted
2 tablespoons light cream

Preheat oven to 425°F.

Into a mixing bowl, sift together the flour, salt, cocoa, and confectioner's sugar. Cut the shortening into the mixture with a pastry blender until the mixture looks like coarse meal. Add the ice water, 1 tablespoon at a time. Gather the dough into a ball, wrap in wax paper, and chill for 1 hour.

Roll out on a lightly floured board until ⅛ inch thick. Place in pie plate and trim.

To make the Inside Stuff: In the large bowl of an electric mixer, beat the eggs until light. Add the sugar, salt, nutmeg, milk, and vanilla, and beat until smooth. Pour into the prepared shell and bake in preheated oven for 15 minutes, then reduce the oven temperature to 350°F. and continue to bake for about 30 minutes more. Pie is done when knife inserted into pie comes out clean. Cool pie completely before adding the finishing touch.

To make the Finishing Touch: In the top of a double boiler over hot but not boiling water, melt the chocolate and butter. Remove from heat. Beat in the sugar and cream. Beat until smooth, then spread on top of pie.

Serves 7–8.

Mocha Parfait Pie

When you have sweet thoughts, this is the solution.

9-inch pie plate, buttered

Crust:
1½ cups crushed chocolate cookies
 1 stick butter, melted
 1 teaspoon instant coffee

Filling:
 2 tablespoons instant coffee
 2 tablespoons dark brown sugar
 1 tablespoon boiling water
⅓ cup plus 2 teaspoons dark rum
1½ quarts vanilla ice cream
 1 cup whipping cream
   Bittersweet chocolate, grated

Blend together the crushed cookies, butter, and coffee. Pat onto the bottom and sides of the pie plate. Chill.

To make the filling: In a small mixing bowl, combine the coffee with the sugar, add the boiling water, and stir until dissolved.

Put the ice cream into the chilled bowl of an electric mixer, add the coffee mixture and ⅓ cup of rum and whip until blended, without allowing ice cream to melt.

Spoon the ice cream mixture into the prepared crust and freeze.

Whip the cream with the 2 teaspoons of the rum.

To serve, decorate with the whipped flavored cream and garnish with the grated chocolate.

Serves 8–10.

Mocha-Choc Chiffon Pie

The combination of coffee and chocolate is one of my favorites.

9-inch pastry shell, baked and cooled

Filling:
- 1 tablespoon gelatin
- ¼ cup cold water
- ½ cup sugar
- 2 squares (2 ounces) bitter chocolate
- ½ cup hot milk
- ½ cup extra-strong coffee
- ¼ teaspoon salt
- 1 teaspoon vanilla
- 1 cup whipping cream, whipped
- 1 cup whipping cream
- 3 tablespoons sugar
- 1 tablespoon Kahlua
- ½ cup ground toasted almonds
- Bitter chocolate, grated

Soften the gelatin in the cold water until dissolved.

In a saucepan, combine the ½ cup of sugar, 2 squares of chocolate, hot milk, coffee, and salt, and bring to a boil, stirring until all the ingredients are well blended. Add the gelatin to this mixture. Remove from heat, cool, and stir in 1 teaspoon of vanilla. Refrigerate.

When cold, fold in the cup of whipped cream. Spoon into the prepared shell and chill for 2–3 hours.

Whip the cream with the sugar and Kahlua.

Decorate the pie with the toasted almonds topped with grated bitter chocolate and serve with the sweetened, Kahlua-flavored whipped cream.

Serves 8.

Velvet Chiffon Pie

For extra pizzazz, pour this filling into this chocolate crust.

9-inch pie plate, buttered

Chocolate Crust:

1½ cups flour
4 tablespoons cocoa
3 tablespoons confectioner's sugar
½ teaspoon salt
½ cup shortening
3 tablespoons ice water

Filling:

1 tablespoon gelatin
¼ cup cold water
½ cup boiling water
6 tablespoons cocoa
4 eggs, separated
1 cup sugar plus additional as needed
¼ teaspoon salt
1½ teaspoons vanilla
1 cup whipping cream

Preheat oven to 450°F.

To make the crust: Into a mixing bowl, sift the flour, cocoa, sugar, and salt. Cut the shortening into the mixture with a pastry blender until the mixture looks like coarse meal. Add the the ice water, 1 tablespoon at a time. Blend briefly.

Gather the dough into a ball, wrap in wax paper, and chill about 1 hour.

Roll out on a lightly floured board to about ⅛ inch thick, and fit into the pan. Prick the bottom of the crust with a fork in several places to prevent buckling.

Bake in preheated oven about 12 minutes. Allow to cool.

To make the filling: Soften the gelatin in the cold water. Mix the boiling water with the cocoa and stir until smooth. Add the gelatin mixture and stir until dissolved. Beat the egg yolks with ½ cup of sugar, salt, and vanilla, and add to the hot mixture.

Cook the custard in a saucepan over medium heat until the mixture begins to thicken. Remove from heat and cool.

On a large open platter, beat the egg whites with the remaining ½ cup of sugar until stiff but not dry, and fold them into the cooled custard. Spoon into the baked, cooled shell and refrigerate until set.

Whip the cream with sugar to taste.

Garnish with sweetened whipped cream.

Serves 6–8.

Gingered Rum Chocolate Pie

When you like chocolate and rum, you incorporate the two whenever
you can, as in this delicious pie.

9-inch pie plate, buttered

Crust:

14–16 gingersnaps, crushed
  5–6 tablespoons butter, melted

Filling:

  1¼ cups milk
   2 eggs, beaten
  ½ cup sugar
  3½ tablespoons cornstarch
  1½ squares (1½ ounces) bitter chocolate, melted
   1 teaspoon vanilla
   2 tablespoons rum
  ¾ cup whipping cream

Preheat oven to 300°F.

Combine the crushed gingersnaps and butter until well blended,
then pat onto the bottom and sides of the pie pan. Bake for 10 minutes
in preheated oven. Cool.

To make the filling: In the top of a double boiler, scald the milk.
Pour a bit of the milk into the eggs, beating constantly. Then slowly
add the beaten eggs to the milk mixture.

Combine the sugar and cornstarch and stir into the egg mixture.
Cook, stirring frequently, for 15–20 minutes, until the custard coats
the back of a spoon. Mix ⅓ of the hot custard with the melted
chocolate and stir until cool, then add vanilla.

Let the balance of the custard cool; stir once in a while to prevent
lumping. When room temperature, add 1 tablespoon of the rum.

Spoon the cooled chocolate filling into the prepared crust, gently
add the cooled rum custard, and chill.

Whip the cream with the remaining 1 tablespoon of rum.

To serve, cover with whipped cream and top with grated chocolate.
Serves 8–10.

Fresh Strawberry Pie

A lovely way to welcome spring's luscious fruit.

10-inch baked pastry shell, cooled and lined with melted
  semisweet chocolate. Refrigerate until ready to fill.

½ cup extra-fine sugar
 5 cups fresh strawberries, washed, dried, and stemmed
 1 cup water
 2 tablespoons cornstarch
¾ cup plus 2 tablespoons granulated sugar
 1 tablespoon grated orange zest
 1 cup whipping cream
    Bitter chocolate, grated

Combine the extra-fine sugar with 4 cups of the strawberries. Let
stand for about 1 hour, then drain the juice.

Crush the remaining cup of strawberries, place in a saucepan with
the water, and bring to a boil. Reduce heat and cook for 2 minutes.

Blend the cornstarch with the ¾ cup of granulated sugar. Add to
juice drawn from sugared berries and stir until smooth. Blend into the
crushed berries and cook, stirring until slightly thick and clear. Add
the orange zest, then let cool.

Place the drained berries stem end down in prepared shell. Spoon
the sauce over all.

Whip the cream, adding the 2 tablespoons of sugar. Garnish with
the whipped cream and grated bitter chocolate. Refrigerate.

Serves 8–10.

Chocolate Cherry Pie

For serious desserting, try this.

9-inch pie plate, buttered

Pastry Shell:

1½ cups flour

½ teaspoon salt

½ cup shortening

3 tablespoons ice water

Filling:

2 tablespoons flour

2 tablespoons cornstarch

½ teaspoon salt

¾ cup sugar

2 cups milk

2 squares (2 ounces) bitter chocolate, grated

3 egg yolks

1 teaspoon vanilla

1 tablespoon butter

2 tablespoons dark rum

½ cup maraschino cherries, drained and quartered

1½ cups whipping cream, whipped

2 tablespoons confectioner's sugar

Bitter chocolate, grated

Preheat oven to 450°F.

Sift the flour and salt into a mixing bowl. Cut the shortening into the mixture with a pastry blender until the mixture looks like coarse meal. Add the ice water, 1 tablespoon at a time.

Gather the dough into a ball, wrap in wax paper, and chill for 1 hour.

Roll out on a lightly floured board until ⅛ inch thick. Fit into the pie pan, prick the bottom with a fork, and bake in preheated oven for about 12 minutes. Allow to cool.

To make the filling: In a saucepan, combine the dry ingredients, add the milk and chocolate, and bring to a boil. Lower the heat and cook, stirring constantly, until thickened.

Lightly beat the egg yolks and add slowly to the custard, stirring over low heat for 2–3 minutes. Add the vanilla, rum, and butter and cool to room temperature. Lastly, whip ½ cup of the cream and fold in the cherries. Spoon into prebaked shell and chill.

Whip the remaining 1 cup of whipping cream with the confectioner's sugar.

To serve, decorate with sweetened whipped cream and grated bitter chocolate.

Serves 8.

Mocha Chocolate Walnut Pie

The crust makes the difference here, the brown sugar and walnuts adding an unusual flavor.

9-inch pie plate

Crust:

1 cup flour, sifted
¼ cup light brown sugar
½ teaspoon salt
6 tablespoons cold butter, chipped
⅓ cup chopped walnuts
1 square (1 ounce) bitter chocolate, grated
1 tablespoon cold water
1 teaspoon vanilla

Filling:

1½ sticks butter
1¼ cups confectioner's sugar
3 eggs
2 squares (2 ounces) bitter chocolate, melted
2 teaspoons instant coffee

Topping:

1 cup whipping cream
1½ tablespoons cocoa
3 tablespoons sugar
1 square (1 ounce) semisweet chocolate, grated

Preheat oven to 350°F.

Combine the sifted flour with the sugar and salt. Blend in the butter, walnuts, and chocolate. Add the water and vanilla, and work dough until it holds together. Roll out on a lightly floured board to ⅛ inch thick and line pie pan. Bake in preheated oven until brown, about 12–15 minutes. Remove and cool.

To make the filling: Cream the butter with the sugar until light. Add the eggs, 1 at a time, beating well after each addition. Blend in the melted chocolate and instant coffee. Spoon the filling into the baked pie shell and chill for at least 1 hour.

To make the topping: Whip the cream with the cocoa and sugar until stiff. Spread evenly over pie and sprinkle with grated semisweet chocolate.

Serves 8–10.

Fresh Raspberry Pie

2 8-inch chocolate crumb crusts

or

2 8-inch pastry shells

Semisweet chocolate, melted

1 cup heavy cream

2 egg whites

1½ cups fresh raspberries

or

10-ounce package frozen raspberries

1¼ cups sugar

or

1 cup sugar if using frozen raspberries

1 tablespoon lemon juice

Coat the crusts or pastry shells with the semisweet chocolate. Refrigerate.

Whip the cream until stiff, then set aside.

In a large open platter, beat the egg whites until fluffy. Add the raspberries, sugar, and lemon juice, and continue to beat on high speed for about 12–15 minutes.

Fold the whipped cream into the berry mixture and spoon into prepared shells. Freeze about 3 hours.

Each pie will serve 8.

COOKIES, BROWNIES, AND SQUARES

COOKIES
Miss Grimble's Butter Cookies
Chocolate Almond Florentines
Chocolate Meringue Cookies
Fruit and Nut Kisses
Cereal Crunchies
Oatmeal Drops
Cocoa Oatmeal Drop Cookies
Chocolate Spritz Cookies
Chocolate Nut Log Cookies
Fudge Wafers
Chocolate Nut Dainties
Choco Macaroons

Chocolate Nests
Dr Pepper Chocolate Yum Yums
Fancy Spice Cookies
Little Ginger Men
New England Marble Cookies
Chocolate Crisps
Chocolate and Vanilla Pinwheels
Nuggets

BROWNIES AND SQUARES AND MORE
Honey Brownies
Double Chocolate Brownies
Nut 'n' Raisin Brownies
Chocolate Mallow Brownies
Chocolate Bourbon Squares
Coconut Marble Squares
Mocha-Iced Chocolate Squares
Molasses Squares
Milk Chocolate-y Bars
Semisweet Bars
Chocolate Mint Sticks

Cookies

Miss Grimble's Butter Cookies

These are very popular.

Greased cookie sheet

- 1 stick butter, softened
- 1⅓ cups sugar
- 3 eggs
- 3 tablespoons orange juice
- Grated rind of 1 orange
- ½ teaspoon vanilla
- 2 cups flour
- ¼ teaspoon salt
- 6–12 ounces semisweet chocolate bits

Preheat oven to 375°F.

In a large bowl, cream the butter until light and lemony. Blend in the sugar and eggs, and beat well. Add the orange juice, grated rind, and vanilla, and beat to blend. Gradually add the flour and salt and mix thoroughly.

Drop by teaspoonfuls on the prepared cookie sheet, about 1½ inches apart, and bake about 15 minutes.

Transfer to a rack and cool.

In the top of a double boiler over hot water, melt the chocolate bits. Cool.

Dip or sprinkle chocolate on the cookies in a circular pattern or any design that suits your fancy.

Makes 4 dozen.

Chocolate Almond Florentines

I can resist anything but temptation—and this is temptation!

Cookie sheet, buttered

½ cup sugar
⅓ cup light cream
⅓ cup light corn syrup
2 tablespoons butter
¼ cup flour, sifted
1 cup blanched coarsely grated almonds
⅓ cup diced candied orange peel

Chocolate Icing:

2½ squares (2½ ounces) semisweet chocolate
3 tablespoons extra-strong coffee
1 tablespoon butter

Preheat oven to 375°F.

In a saucepan, combine the sugar, cream, syrup, and butter over low heat until sugar is dissolved. Increase the heat and boil until the temperature reaches 238°F. on a candy thermometer.

Remove from heat and add the sifted flour, grated almonds, and diced orange peel. Blend well and drop by teaspoonfuls onto the prepared cookie sheet, about 2½ inches apart. Bake in preheated oven for 8–10 minutes. The cookies will be browned. Remove from oven and cool 1–2 minutes, until set enough to lift from pan. Remove from pan and place on rack to cool.

To make the icing: In a saucepan, combine the chocolate, coffee, and butter over low heat, stirring until the chocolate is dissolved. Remove from heat and place a teaspoon or more on top of each florentine to ice. Chocolate will set.

Makes about 24–26 cookies.

Chocolate Meringue Cookies

Very simple and worth the effort!

Cookie sheet, lightly oiled

3 egg whites
¾ cup extra-fine sugar
3 tablespoons cocoa
1 teaspoon vanilla

Preheat oven to 275°F.

On a large open platter, beat the egg whites until stiff.

Sift the sugar with the cocoa and add gradually to the beaten egg whites. Stir in vanilla and drop the mixture by teaspoonfuls onto the cookie sheet. Bake in preheated oven about 30 minutes, until lightly browned, and remove from cookie sheet while still warm. Cool on rack.

Makes about 2 dozen.

Variation: This can also be used as a shell for a 9-inch pie. In buttered pan, bake shell for 1 hour in preheated oven at 275°F.

Fruit and Nut Kisses

Cookie sheet, oiled

2 egg whites
Pinch salt
1 cup sugar
2 tablespoons cocoa
1 teaspoon vanilla
1 cup chopped nuts (pecans, walnuts, or almonds)
1 cup chopped pitted dates
Confectioner's sugar, sifted

Preheat oven to 250°F.

Whip the egg whites with the salt on a large open platter with a wire beater. Sift together the cocoa and sugar. Add the cocoa and sugar gradually. Add the vanilla and whip until stiff.

Fold in the nuts and dates. Drop by teaspoonfuls onto the cookie sheet and bake in preheated oven until they are almost dry and firm, about 30 minutes. Remove from sheet while hot.

Cool and dust with sifted confectioner's sugar.

Makes 3½ dozen.

Cereal Crunchies

You can use orange juice in place of the vanilla as a flavoring.

Cookie sheet, buttered and floured

1 stick butter or ½ cup shortening
1 cup packed dark brown sugar
1 egg
½ cup flour
¼ teaspoon salt
  Grated rind of 1 orange
1¼ teaspoons vanilla
1½ cups rolled oats
7 ounces semisweet chocolate bits

Preheat oven to 375°F.

In a large bowl, cream the butter or shortening and the sugar until light, then add the egg and beat well. Sift the flour before measuring and blend with the salt. Beat into the butter mixture with the rind and vanilla. Add the oatmeal and chocolate bits. Mix well. Drop by teaspoonfuls onto the prepared cookie sheet. Bake in preheated oven for 15–18 minutes, until lightly brown.

Makes 4 dozen.

Oatmeal Drops

Nice and crunchy, these aren't your typical oatmeal cookie.

Cookie sheet, buttered

½ cup shortening
⅔ cup sugar
2 eggs
¼ cup plus 2 tablespoons milk
2 squares (2 ounces) bitter chocolate, melted
1 cup flour
1 teaspoon baking powder
1 teaspoon cinnamon
½ teaspoon nutmeg
½ teaspoon salt
1 cup rolled oats

Preheat oven to 350°F.

In a large bowl, cream together the shortening and the sugar until light.

Beat the eggs and add to the shortening mixture with the milk and melted chocolate.

Sift together the flour, baking powder, cinnamon, nutmeg, and salt. Mix with the oats, then add to the batter. Mix well.

Drop by teaspoonfuls onto the prepared cookie sheet and bake for 20 minutes, until lightly brown.

Makes 2½ dozen.

Cocoa Oatmeal Drop Cookies

This is about the only way most people will eat oatmeal—in a chocolate cookie!

Cookie sheet, buttered

1½ sticks butter or ¾ cup shortening
1 cup dark brown sugar
3 tablespoons dark corn syrup
1 cup flour
½ teaspoon salt
2 teaspoons baking powder
½ teaspoon cinnamon
½ teaspoon allspice
2 tablespoons cocoa
¾ cup milk
2 cups 3-minute oats
½ cup raisins
½ cup chopped nuts

Preheat oven to 375°F.

In a large bowl, cream together the butter or shortening and the sugar until light. Add the syrup.

Sift together the flour, salt, baking powder, cinnamon, allspice, and cocoa, and combine alternately with milk to the butter mixture. Add the oatmeal, raisins, and nuts, and blend well. Chill for about 45 minutes.

Drop by teaspoonfuls onto the prepared cookie sheet and bake in preheated oven for 8–10 minutes, until lightly brown.

Makes 2½ dozen.

Chocolate Spritz Cookies

Cookie sheet, buttered

½ cup shortening
¾ cup sugar
1½ squares (1½ ounces) bitter chocolate, melted
2 teaspoons milk
1 egg
½ teaspoon vanilla
½ teaspoon almond extract
1¾ cup flour
½ teaspoon baking powder

Preheat oven to 400°F.

In a large bowl, cream together the shortening and the sugar. Add the melted chocolate and milk. Blend.

Beat the egg and add to the mixture. Add the vanilla and almond flavoring.

Sift together the flour and baking powder; stir in. Mix well. Put through a cookie press onto the prepared cookie sheet. Or wrap in wax paper, chill, roll out ¼ inch thick on floured board, and cut with round cutter. Place on prepared cookie sheet.

Bake for 8 minutes, until browned.

Makes 3 dozen.

Chocolate Nut Log Cookies

Cookie sheet, buttered

2 squares (2 ounces) bitter chocolate
1 stick butter or ½ cup shortening
1½ cups sugar
1 egg
¾ teaspoon vanilla
2½ cups flour
½ teaspoon salt
1 teaspoon baking powder
¼ cup milk
½ cup toasted slivered almonds

Preheat oven to 400°F.

In the top of a double boiler over hot but not boiling water, melt the chocolate and cool.

In a large bowl, combine the butter or shortening and sugar, and cream until light. Add the egg, chocolate, and vanilla, and beat again.

Sift the flour before measuring and resift with the salt and baking powder. Add alternately with the milk to the chocolate mixture. Blend well and add the almonds.

Roll the dough into a 2-inch log, wrap in wax paper, and refrigerate overnight.

Slice the cookies less than ¼ inch thick, if possible, and place on prepared cookie sheet. The dough may also be rolled on a lightly floured board and cut with a cookie cutter, then placed on prepared cookie sheet. Bake for 8–10 minutes, until browned.

Makes 4½ dozen.

Fudge Wafers

A wonderful gift idea.

Cookie sheet, buttered

2 sticks butter, softened
1 cup sugar
1 egg
2 squares (2 ounces) bitter chocolate, melted
1 tablespoon vanilla
1½ cups flour, sifted
¼ teaspoon salt
1 cup Brazil nuts, sliced

Preheat oven to 400°F.

In a large bowl, cream the butter. Add the sugar and egg, and beat until light and creamy. Add the melted chocolate and vanilla, and blend well.

Sift together the dry ingredients; add and mix well.

Drop by teaspoonfuls onto prepared cookie sheet. Press a slice of Brazil nut into the center of each cookie. Bake in preheated oven for 8–10 minutes, until browned.

Store in airtight containers.

Makes about 7 dozen.

Chocolate Nut Dainties

These are an elegant addition to any dessert table.

Cookie sheet, buttered

1 egg
½ cup packed dark brown sugar
1½ cups flour, sifted
½ teaspoon salt
½ cup sour milk (½ cup milk plus 1 teaspoon lemon juice)
½ teaspoon baking soda
2½ squares (2½ ounces) bitter chocolate
1 teaspoon vanilla
½ cup chopped nuts

Frosting:
1½ cups confectioner's sugar, sifted
2 tablespoons cocoa
2 tablespoons light cream
2 tablespoons butter

Preheat oven to 350°F.

In a large bowl, beat the egg with the sugar until light.

Sift together the flour, salt, and baking soda, and blend in with the sour milk.

In the top of a double boiler over hot but not boiling water, melt the chocolate, add with vanilla and nuts to the batter. Mix well.

Drop by teaspoonfuls onto the prepared cookie sheet and bake for 10–12 minutes, until browned. Frost while hot.

To make the frosting: Combine the confectioner's sugar, cocoa, cream, and butter. Beat until smooth, then frost cookies.

Makes 3 dozen.

Choco Macaroons

Always a hit.

Cookie sheet, buttered

⅔ cup sweetened condensed milk
1 teaspoon vanilla
2 cups shredded coconut
6 ounces semisweet chocolate bits

Preheat oven to 350°F.

In a large bowl, combine all ingredients and mix well.

Drop by teaspoonfuls 1 inch apart onto prepared cookie sheet. Bake about 10 minutes. Remove immediately from sheet.

Makes 2½ dozen.

Chocolate Nests

You can freeze these, and then they won't get eaten all at once.

Cookie sheet, buttered

1 cup sugar
½ cup water
1 pound unblanched slivered almonds
5 egg whites
Pinch salt
1 teaspoon vanilla
1 pound confectioner's sugar
4 squares (4 ounces) bitter chocolate, melted

Preheat oven to 300°F.

In a large saucepan, combine the sugar and water, and cook until syrup spins a thread, when the temperature on a candy thermometer reaches 234°F. Stir in the nuts slowly and continue stirring until all the syrup is absorbed.

On a large open platter, beat the egg whites until frothy. Add salt and vanilla, and continue beating until the whites are very stiff. Gradually beat in the confectioner's sugar. Fold in the nuts and melted chocolate. Drop by teaspoonfuls onto the prepared cookie sheet and bake for 20–25 minutes, until browned. For half the quantity, divide ingredient amounts by 2.

Makes 10 dozen.

Dr Pepper Chocolate Yum Yums

Another Dr Pepper goodie that children love. Since they are re-frigerator cookies, they can be baked a few at a time as needed.

Cookie sheet, lightly buttered

- 1 stick butter, softened
- 1¼ cups sugar
- 1 egg
- 2 squares (2 ounces) bitter chocolate, melted and slightly cooled
- 2 cups flour
- ¼ teaspoon baking powder
- ¼ teaspoon salt
- ¼ cup Dr Pepper
- 2 teaspoons vanilla
- 1 cup chopped walnuts

Preheat oven to 375°F.

In a large bowl, cream the butter, add the sugar, and beat until light and fluffy. Add the egg and beat hard. Blend in the cooled and melted chocolate.

Sift the dry ingredients together and add to the creamed mixture alternately with the Dr Pepper, starting with the flour, then the Dr Pepper, and finally the remaining half of the flour. Mix slowly.

Add the vanilla and nuts, blend well, and spread on wax paper. Form into 2-inch roll, wrap in foil, and chill in refrigerator until ready to bake. Slice to desired thickness, place on cookie sheet, and bake in preheated oven for 10–12 minutes, until browned.

Makes 3–3½ dozen (about ¼-inch) cookies.

Fancy Spice Cookies

Another refrigerator cookie—good for doing ahead.

Cookie sheet, buttered

- 1 cup shortening
- 1 cup sugar
- 1 square (1 ounce) bitter chocolate, melted
- 2 eggs
- 1¼ teaspoons vanilla
- 3½ cups flour
- ½ teaspoon baking powder
- ½ teaspoon salt
- 2 teaspoons cinnamon
- ½ teaspoon nutmeg

Preheat oven to 350°F.

In a large bowl, cream the shortening and the sugar together. Add the melted chocolate and eggs, 1 at a time, beating well after each addition. Add the vanilla.

Sift all the dry ingredients together, add, and mix well. Wrap in wax paper and chill until firm.

Roll out on a floured board to about ¼ inch thick and cut into 2-inch squares. Place on prepared cookie sheet and bake for 15 minutes, until browned.

Makes 3 dozen.

Little Ginger Men

Manufacturers now make gingerbread men cutters as small as one inch. The shorter the "men," the more cookies, of course.

Cookie sheet, buttered

½ cup shortening
½ cup molasses
2 squares (2 ounces) bitter chocolate
2½ cups flour
⅔ cup sugar
1 teaspoon baking powder
½ teaspoon baking soda
1 teaspoon ground ginger
¼ teaspoon salt
¼ cup milk
½ cup frosting (see pp. 42–45)
   or
   confectioner's sugar

Preheat oven to 375°F.

In the top of a double boiler over hot but not boiling water, combine the shortening, molasses, and chocolate. Heat, stirring, until blended. Cool.

Sift together the flour, sugar, baking powder, baking soda, ground ginger, and salt; add to the chocolate mixture. Add the milk and mix well. Chill until firm, then roll out ⅛ inch thick on a floured board and cut in the shape of gingerbread men. Bake on prepared cookie sheet for 6 minutes, until browned. Decorate with frosting or confectioner's sugar.

Makes 2 dozen.

New England Marble Cookies

Kids love the way these look—and taste.

Cookie sheet, buttered

½ cup shortening
⅔ cup sugar
1 teaspoon vanilla
1¼ cups flour
5 teaspoons milk
1 square (1 ounce) bitter chocolate, melted

Preheat oven to 350°F.

In a large bowl, cream the shortening and sugar together. Add the vanilla and flour, and mix well. Divide the dough in half.

Add milk to half of the dough and melted chocolate to the other half. Mix each half well.

Roll the vanilla dough into an oblong ⅛ inch thick on a lightly floured board. Do the same with the chocolate dough. Place the chocolate dough on top of the vanilla dough, press together, and roll up jelly-roll fashion. Cut in half, then shape into 2 rolls 2 inches in diameter and wrap in wax paper. Chill until firm.

Slice ¼ inch thick. Place on prepared cookie sheet and bake for 12 minutes, until marbled.

Makes 3 dozen.

Chocolate Crisps

Cookie sheet, buttered

½ cup shortening
1 cup sugar
3 squares (3 ounces) bitter chocolate
2 eggs
1 teaspoon vanilla
2¼ cups flour
¾ teaspoon baking soda
½ teaspoon salt

Preheat oven to 375°F.

Cream the shortening and sugar. Melt the chocolate over hot water. Beat the eggs and add the chocolate and eggs to butter mixture. Add the vanilla. Sift together the flour, soda, and salt and add to mixture.

Wrap in wax paper. Chill until firm. Roll out ⅛ inch thick on lightly floured board.

Cut in 1 × 3-inch strips. Place on prepared cookie sheet and bake for 10 minutes.

Makes 6 dozen.

Chocolate and Vanilla Pinwheels

Follow recipe for chocolate crisps and then do the following:

Cookie sheet, buttered

½ cup shortening
1 cup sugar
2 eggs
2 tablespoons milk
1½ teaspoons vanilla
2¾ cups flour
2 teaspoons baking powder
1 teaspoon salt
¼ cup shredded coconut or ¼ cup chopped nuts

Preheat oven to 375°F.

Cream together the shortening and the sugar. Beat 2 eggs and add. Add the milk and vanilla. Sift together the flour, baking powder, and salt, then add and mix well.

Wrap in wax paper and chill until firm.

Remove both doughs—the chocolate crisp and the vanilla. Unwrap and roll in oblongs 8 × 15 × ⅛ inch on wax paper. Place chocolate dough on vanilla dough and press together. Sprinkle with coconut or nuts. Trim edges and roll up jelly-roll fashion. Wrap in wax paper and chill until firm.

Slice ¼ inch thick and place on prepared cookie sheet. Bake for 12 minutes.

Makes 7 dozen.

Nuggets

Cookie sheet, buttered

2 cups butter, margarine or shortening
  or
2 sticks butter and 1 cup margarine
  or
2 sticks butter and 1 cup shortening
2 cups packed brown sugar
1 teaspoon cinnamon
¼ teaspoon nutmeg
2 eggs
3 cups flour
1½ teaspoons baking powder
1½ teaspoons salt
½ cup sour cream
½ cup sweet chocolate, grated
1½ cups chopped walnuts or pecans
1 cup seedless raisins

Preheat oven to 350°F.

In a large bowl, combine the shortening, sugar, and spices, and cream until light and lemony. Add the eggs and beat again.

Sift the flour before measuring and resift with the baking powder and salt. Add to the butter mixture, alternating with sour cream. Add the chocolate and blend well. Add the nuts and raisins, and mix well. Drop by teaspoonfuls onto prepared cookie sheet.

Bake in preheated oven for 15 minutes. Remove from pan and cool.
Makes 4½ dozen.

Brownies and Squares and More

Honey Brownies

A very harmonious blending of flavors.

---

7 × 11-inch pan, buttered and lightly floured

½ cup shortening
½ cup dark corn syrup
½ cup honey
2 eggs, beaten
½ cup flour
¼ teaspoon baking soda
⅛ teaspoon salt
2 squares (2 ounces) bitter chocolate, melted
½ cup chopped walnuts

Preheat oven to 300°F.

In a bowl, cream the shortening, then add the corn syrup, honey, and beaten eggs.

Sift the dry ingredients and add to the mixture with the melted chocolate and walnuts. When well blended, spoon into prepared pan and bake for 45 minutes.

Cool and cut into small squares.
Serves 6.

Double Chocolate Brownies

As a variation, leave the brownies unfrosted and sprinkle with confectioner's sugar when cool.

8-inch square pan, buttered

2 eggs
  Pinch salt
1 cup sugar
2½ squares (2½ ounces) bitter chocolate
1 stick butter
1 teaspoon vanilla
½ cup flour, sifted
1 cup chopped pecans

Frosting:
1 tablespoon butter
¾ cup confectioner's sugar
2 tablespoons cocoa
2 tablespoons milk or light cream
½ teaspoon vanilla

Preheat oven to 350°F.

Beat the eggs with the pinch of salt until lemony. Add the sugar and mix well.

In the top of a double boiler over hot water, melt the chocolate and butter together, and add to the egg mixture. Add the vanilla, sifted flour, and pecans. Pour into prepared pan and bake for 20 minutes. Frost and cut while hot. Cool before removing from pan.

To make the frosting: Cream together the butter, sugar, and cocoa. Blend in the milk or cream and vanilla, and mix until smooth.

Serves 6–8.

Nut 'n' Raisin Brownies

This is a very rich brownie!

8-inch square pan, buttered

1 stick butter
1 cup sugar
2 eggs
2 squares (2 ounces) bitter chocolate
½ cup chopped nuts
½ cup seedless raisins
¾ teaspoon vanilla
½ cup flour
Pinch salt
½–1 cup frosting (see pp. 42–45)
    or
confectioner's sugar

Preheat oven to 350°F.

In a large bowl, combine the butter and sugar and cream well. Add eggs and beat again.

In the top of a double boiler over hot water, melt the chocolate. Add the chocolate, nuts, and raisins to the butter mixture. Add the vanilla.

Sift together the flour and salt, then add slowly, mixing well. Pour into prepared cake pan and bake in preheated oven for about 20–25 minutes.

Frost while hot, or cool and dust with confectioner's sugar.
Serves 6–8.

Chocolate Mallow Brownies

Another winning combination—chocolate and marshmallow.

8-inch square pan, buttered

½ cup sugar
⅓ cup plus 1 teaspoon shortening
3 tablespoons water
12 ounces semisweet chocolate bits
1 teaspoon vanilla
2 eggs
1 cup flour, sifted
¼ teaspoon baking soda
½ teaspoon salt
½ cup chopped nuts
2 cups miniature marshmallows

Preheat oven to 325°F.

Combine the sugar, ⅓ cup of shortening, and water in a pan, bring to a boil, then remove from heat. Add 1 cup of the chocolate bits and vanilla. Stir until smooth.

Beat in the eggs, 1 at a time, beating until well blended.

Resift the flour with the baking soda and salt, and add to mixture. Add the nuts and blend. Turn into buttered pan and bake for 25 minutes.

Upon removing from the oven, immediately cover the top with the marshmallows. Cool the brownies in the pan. In the top of a double boiler over hot water, melt the remaining cup of chocolate bits with 1 teaspoon of shortening and pour over marshmallows, spreading evenly. Chill and cut into 1½-inch squares.

Makes 2 dozen.

Chocolate Bourbon Squares

These are wonderfully rich.

---

10 × 12-inch pan, lined with wax paper

2 tablespoons butter
¾ cup sugar
4 eggs
1½ cups flour, sifted
1 teaspoon baking powder
1½ tablespoons bourbon whiskey
½ cup unsulphured molasses
¼ teaspoon ground allspice
¼ teaspoon ground cloves
1¼ teaspoons cinnamon
1½ squares (1½ ounces) dark sweet chocolate, grated
¼ cup chopped orange rind
¼ cup chopped lemon rind
1 cup chopped pecans or almonds

Frosting:
1 cup chocolate frosting (see pp. 42–45)
or
1½ cups confectioner's sugar, 2½ tablespoons light
cream, and 2½ tablespoons lemon juice or bourbon

Preheat oven to 350°F.

In a large bowl, cream the butter and sugar until light, then add the eggs, 1 at a time, beating well after each addition.

Resift the flour with the baking powder. Blend all ingredients and spread the mixture in the prepared pan. Bake in preheated oven just until batter begins to leave the sides of the pan, about 30 minutes. Cool slightly.

Frost with any chocolate frosting or combine the confectioner's sugar with cream and lemon juice or bourbon to spreading consistency and frost. Cut into squares.

Serves 10–12.

Coconut Marble Squares

15 × 10-inch pan, buttered

2½ squares (2½ ounces) bitter chocolate
1 cup sugar
⅓ cup hot water
2 cups flour
1 teaspoon baking powder
½ teaspoon salt
1½ sticks butter
1 cup brown sugar, packed
3 eggs
2 tablespoons milk
1 teaspoon vanilla
1 cup shredded coconut

Frosting:
1 cup chocolate frosting (see pp. 42–45)
   or
   confectioner's sugar

Preheat oven to 375°F.

In the top of a double boiler over hot water, melt the chocolate with ¼ cup of the sugar and ⅓ cup hot water. Cool.

Sift the flour with the baking powder and salt.

Cream the butter and gradually add the remaining ¾ cup of sugar and the brown sugar. Add the eggs, 1 at a time, beating well after each addition. Add the milk and vanilla.

Blend in the dry ingredients and mix thoroughly. Add the coconut. Spread this mixture on prepared pan. Pour the chocolate mixture over the top and cut through the batter with a knife in a swirling pattern. Bake for 25 minutes.

Frost while hot and serve when cold. Or serve plain, dusted with confectioner's sugar.

Serves 10–12.

Mocha-Iced Chocolate Squares

When Miss Grimble was still in its infancy, we hired a European baker and his wife, just off the boat, who could not speak one word of English. We taught him to bake our products by just watching. Because he had been baking for his family since he was eight years old, it was child's play for him. This is one of his special chocolate recipes. I cannot tell whether it is of Romanian, Hungarian, or Yugoslavian origin.

8-inch square pan, buttered and dusted with cocoa

½ cup sugar
4 tablespoons butter, softened
5 eggs, separated
2 squares (2 ounces) bitter chocolate, melted
1 tablespoon cocoa
⅓ cup flour
3–4 tablespoons ground walnuts

Filling:
½ cup thick apricot preserves or jam
2–3 tablespoons rum

Topping:
2 tablespoons butter, softened
1 tablespoon cocoa
1¼ cups confectioner's sugar, sifted
2 tablespoons extra-strong coffee
½ teaspoon rum

Preheat oven to 350°F.

In the large bowl of an electric mixer, combine ¼ cup of the sugar and the butter, and beat until light, then add the yolks and continue to beat until blended. Stir in the melted chocolate and cocoa.

On a large open platter, beat the egg whites until stiff, gradually adding the remaining ¼ cup of sugar. Fold gently into the yolk mixture, adding the flour and walnuts.

Spoon the mixture into prepared pan and bake in preheated oven for 20–25 minutes, until top springs back and batter begins to shrink from sides of the pan. Remove from oven and allow to cool. Split cake into two layers.

To make the filling: Stir together the preserves or jam and the rum, and spread on one layer. Top with the other layer.

To make the topping: Blend together the butter, cocoa, confectioner's sugar, coffee, and rum until of spreading consistency. Cover top and sides of cake. Cut into squares.

Serves 8–10.

Molasses Squares

Molasses, chocolate, and pecans just go together.

8-inch square pan, buttered

2½ squares (2½ ounces) bitter chocolate
6 tablespoons butter
½ cup sugar
½ cup unsulphured molasses
2 eggs, beaten
½ teaspoon vanilla
⅔ cup flour, sifted
½ teaspoon baking powder
  Pinch salt
⅓ cup chopped pecans

Preheat oven to 325°F.

In the top of a double boiler over hot but not boiling water, melt the chocolate and butter together. Add the sugar and molasses. Cool. Add the eggs and vanilla. Beat well.

Resift the flour with the baking powder and salt. Add to the mixture, blending well, then add the nuts.

Pour into prepared pan and bake about 25 minutes, until top springs back and batter begins to shrink from sides of the pan.

Serves 6–8.

Milk Chocolate-y Bars

9-inch square pan, buttered

4 tablespoons butter or margarine
1 cup sugar
1 teaspoon vanilla
2 eggs
¼ cup milk
1 cup flour, sifted
2 tablespoons cocoa
¼ teaspoon salt
½ cup chopped walnuts or pecans

Frosting:
1½ tablespoons cocoa
1 tablespoon milk
¼ teaspoon vanilla
1½ teaspoons butter or margarine, softened
⅔ cup confectioner's sugar, sifted

Preheat oven to 375°F.

Cream the butter to soften. Gradually add the sugar and vanilla, creaming well.

Beat in the eggs, 1 at a time. Stir in the milk.

Sift together the dry ingredients; stir into the creamed mixture. Add the nuts. Spread in prepared pan and bake in preheated oven for 20 minutes. Frost at once.

To make the frosting: Blend all ingredients together and spread over top of cake while hot.

Cool, then cut into bars.

Makes 24.

Semisweet Bars

15 × 10-inch pan, buttered

1¼ cups flour, sifted
¾ teaspoon baking soda
½ teaspoon salt
1¼ cups chopped pitted dates
¾ cups packed dark brown sugar
½ cup water
 1 stick butter
 1 cup semisweet chocolate bits
 2 eggs
½ cup orange juice
½ cup milk
 1 cup chopped walnuts or pecans

Frosting:
1½ cups confectioner's sugar
 2 tablespoons butter, softened
1–2 tablespoons grated orange rind
2–3 tablespoons light cream

Preheat oven to 350°F.

Sift the flour with the baking soda and salt.

In a large saucepan, combine the dates, brown sugar, water, and butter. Cook over low heat, stirring constantly, until the dates soften. Remove from heat.

Stir in the chocolate bits, beat in the eggs, and add the dry ingredients alternately with the orange juice and milk. Blend well and add the nuts.

Pour into prepared pan and bake in preheated oven for 25 minutes. Cool.

To make the frosting: Beat together the confectioner's sugar, butter, orange rind, and cream until spreading consistency. Spread over top. Cut into bars or squares.

Makes 24–36.

Chocolate Mint Sticks

Nothing improves the flavor of chocolate like peppermint.

8-inch square pan, buttered

1   stick butter
1   cup sugar
2   eggs
1   teaspoon vanilla
2   squares (2 ounces) bitter chocolate, melted
½   cup flour
½   cup chopped walnuts

Peppermint Frosting:
1   cup confectioner's sugar
2   tablespoons butter, softened
1   tablespoon light cream
¼–½   teaspoon peppermint extract

Glaze:
1   square (1 ounce) bitter chocolate, melted
1   tablespoon butter

Preheat oven to 350°F.

In a large bowl, cream together the butter and the sugar. Beat in the eggs and the vanilla. Beat well. Blend in the melted, cooled chocolate, flour, and nuts. Pour into prepared pan and bake for 25 minutes. Cool.

To make the frosting: In a small bowl, beat together the confectioner's sugar, butter, cream, and peppermint extract. Spread on cooled cake and allow to set before glazing.

To make the glaze: Beat together the melted chocolate and butter. Spread over the frosting. Chill, then cut into bars.

Makes 24.

FUDGES AND CONFECTIONS

FUDGES
Date and Walnut Fudge
Marmalade-filled Fudge
Chocolate-marbled Fudge
Pistachio Chocolate Fudge
Devil's Chocolate Fudge

CONFECTIONS
Chocolate Divinity
Chocolate Nut Caramels

Fudges

Date and Walnut Fudge

An unusual combination, and the dark brown sugar adds the zip.

8-inch square pan, buttered

1 cup sugar
1 cup packed dark brown sugar
¾ cup milk
2 tablespoons light corn syrup
2 squares (2 ounces) bitter chocolate, chopped
3 tablespoons butter
1 teaspoon vanilla
⅓ cup chopped pitted dates
⅓ cup chopped walnuts

In a saucepan, combine the sugars, milk, corn syrup, and chocolate. Cook slowly over low heat, stirring constantly, until mixture boils. Reduce heat and boil slowly, stirring once in a while, until candy thermometer reaches 236°F—the soft-ball stage. Remove from heat.

Add the butter but do *not* stir. Cool slightly.

Add the vanilla and beat until thick. Sprinkle the dates and nuts into prepared pan and pour in the fudge. Cool and cut into small squares.

Makes 1½ pounds.

Marmalade-filled Fudge

Now this is really different.

Cookie sheet
8 × 10-inch pan

¾ cup flour
¼ teaspoon salt
⅓ cup packed brown sugar
⅓ cup butter
1 cup chopped nuts

Filling:
3 squares (3 ounces) bitter chocolate
¼ cup orange, apricot, or pineapple marmalade
¾ teaspoon vanilla
2 cups confectioner's sugar, sifted
¼ cup light cream

Preheat oven to 400°F.

Sift the flour and salt together and add the brown sugar. Cut in the butter and add the nuts. Toast in the oven on a cookie sheet, stirring once in a while, until golden, about 10 minutes. Cool.

To make the filling: In the top of a double boiler over hot but not boiling water, melt the chocolate. Add the marmalade and vanilla, then the confectioner's sugar with the cream. Beat until smooth.

Spread half of the nut mixture in the unbuttered 8 × 10-inch pan. Spoon in the filling, spreading evenly. Cover with the remaining nut mixture, press firmly, and chill for at least 1 hour. Cut into squares.

Store in the refrigerator.

Makes 24.

Chocolate-marbled Fudge

Very enticing.

8-inch square pan, buttered

2 cups sugar
⅔ cup heavy cream
1 cup milk
¼ cup light corn syrup
¼ teaspoon salt
1 teaspoon vanilla
½ cup chopped semisweet chocolate bits

In a saucepan, combine the sugar, cream, milk, corn syrup, and salt. Cook slowly, stirring constantly, until the mixture boils. Boil slowly, stirring once in a while, until the temperature on a candy thermometer reaches 234°F—the soft-ball stage. Remove from heat.

Cool and add the vanilla. Beat until the mixture thickens. Pour half the mixture into prepared pan. Sprinkle on half the chopped chocolate bits, pour in the rest of the warm mixture, and sprinkle with remaining chocolate bits.

Cool and cut into bars.

Makes 1¼ pounds.

Pistachio Chocolate Fudge

Follow directions and ingredients for Devil's Chocolate Fudge (p. 119). Use ½ teaspoon of vanilla, instead of 1 teaspoon, plus ½ teaspoon of almond extract and ⅔ cup of halved pistachio nuts. Sprinkle nuts on the bottom of a buttered pan, pour in fudge, and cool.

Makes 1½ pounds.

Devil's Chocolate Fudge

Truly devilish!

8-inch square pan, buttered

1 cup sugar
1 cup packed dark brown sugar
¾ cup milk
2 tablespoons light corn syrup
2 squares (2 ounces) bitter chocolate, chopped
3 tablespoons butter
1 teaspoon vanilla

In a saucepan, combine the sugars, milk, corn syrup, and chopped chocolate. Cook slowly over low heat, stirring constantly, until mixture boils. Boil slowly, stirring once in a while, until the temperature on a candy thermometer reaches 236°F—the soft-ball stage. Remove from heat.

Add butter but do *not* stir. Cool slightly, add the vanilla, and beat until thick. Pour into prepared pan. Cool thoroughly, then cut into squares.

Makes 1¼ pounds.

Confections

Chocolate Divinity

If you like divinity, you will like this rendition.

2½ cups sugar
½ cup light corn syrup
½ cup water
¼ teaspoon salt
2 egg whites
2 squares (2 ounces) bitter chocolate, melted and cooled
1 teaspoon vanilla
1 cup chopped pecans

In a saucepan, combine the sugar, corn syrup, water, and salt. Cook over medium heat, stirring constantly, until mixture comes to a boil. Reduce the heat and cook without stirring until the temperature on a candy thermometer reaches 248°F—the firm-ball stage.

Just 1 minute before this temperature is reached, beat the egg whites on a large platter until stiff.

Pour half of the syrup mixture over the beaten whites, slowly, beating constantly until blended. Cook the remaining syrup to 272°F—the thread stage on the candy thermometer. Add the hot syrup mixture to the first mixture, 1 teaspoonful at a time, beating well after each addition with an electric beater. After the last addition, beat about 5 minutes. Add the melted chocolate, vanilla, and nuts. Beat until the mixture loses its gloss and holds its shape when dropped from a spoon—about 5 minutes more. Drop by teaspoonfuls onto wax paper.

Makes 1¼ pounds.

Chocolate Nut Caramels

An easy candy that can be made ahead for any occasion.

8-inch square pan, buttered

1 cup sugar
1 cup packed dark brown sugar
1 cup light corn syrup
1 cup sweetened condensed milk
½ cup light cream
1 cup milk
6 squares (6 ounces) bitter chocolate
2 tablespoons butter
2 teaspoons vanilla
Pinch salt
1½ cups chopped walnuts or pecans

In a saucepan, combine the sugars, corn syrup, condensed milk, cream, and milk, and cook slowly, stirring constantly, until the sugars are dissolved.

In the top of a double boiler over hot water, melt the chocolate and add to the sugar mixture with the butter. Cook slowly, stirring constantly, until the temperature on a candy thermometer reaches 246°F. Remove from heat and add vanilla, salt, and nuts. Blend and pour into prepared pan and cool.

When firm, turn out on a board and cut into squares. Wrap each square in wax paper.

Makes 2½ pounds.

SOUFFLÉS, MOUSSES, AND RUSSES

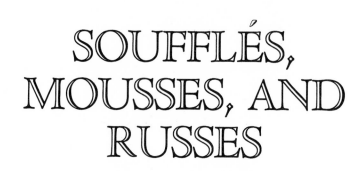

SOUFFLÉS
Black Cherry Soufflé
Sherried Nut Soufflé
Baked Chocolate Meringue Soufflé
Soufflé for Two

MOUSSES
The Decadent Mousse
Italian Chocolate Mousse
Blender Mousse
Cold Cashew Mousse
Armagnac Mousse
Supreme Chocolate Mousse

RUSSES AND MORE

Macaroon Cream Cake

Chocolate Charlotte Russe

Frozen Orange Chocolate Charlotte

Macaroon Rum Charlotte

Chocolate Marshmallow Dessert

Coffee Marshmallow Cream

Black Russian Parfait

Zabaglione Parfait

A Chocolate Mountain

Blender Bavarian Cream

Chocolate Chantilly Crème

Venetian Pot de Crème

Baked Pot de Crème

Chocolate Orange Sponge

Ladyfinger Cake

Soufflés

Black Cherry Soufflé

This soufflé is Italian in origin—simple and delicious.

1-quart baking dish, buttered

½ cup black cherry preserves
4 eggs, separated
2 tablespoons confectioner's sugar
1⅓ tablespoons cocoa

Preheat oven to 425°F.

Spread cherries over the bottom of the buttered baking dish.

On a large open platter, beat the egg whites until stiff. Beat the egg yolks until light and lemony, and gradually add the confectioner's sugar and cocoa, blending thoroughly. Fold in the stiffly beaten whites gently and spoon over the cherries.

Bake near the top of the oven for 15–18 minutes or until the soufflé rises. Remove from oven and serve immediately.

Serves 2.

Sherried Nut Soufflé

A soulful hint of brandy and sherry with chocolate.

2-quart soufflé dish, buttered and dusted with granulated sugar

2½ squares (2½ ounces) bitter chocolate
2 cups milk
½ cup sugar
⅓ cup flour
½ teaspoon salt
2 tablespoons butter
1 teaspoon vanilla
2 tablespoons brandy
2 tablespoons sherry
4 eggs, separated
½ cup finely chopped walnuts

Preheat oven to 350°F.

In the top of a double boiler over hot water, melt the chocolate in the milk, beating with a rotary beater until blended. Sift together the sugar, flour, and salt. Add in small amounts to the chocolate mixture, then cook for about 5 minutes, stirring frequently.

Remove from heat, cool slightly, and add butter, flavorings, and well-beaten egg yolks.

On a large open platter beat the egg whites until stiff and fold gently into the soufflé mixture along with the walnuts.

Spoon into prepared soufflé dish to full. Place in a pan of hot water so that the water reaches halfway up the soufflé dish, and bake in preheated oven for 1 hour or until the soufflé is firm.

Serve immediately.

Serves 8.

Baked Chocolate Meringue Soufflé

7-inch baking dish, buttered

2 tablespoons butter
3 tablespoons flour
1 cup milk
3 squares (3 ounces) bitter chocolate
3 tablespoons hot water
½ cup sugar
¼ teaspoon salt
½ teaspoon vanilla
3 eggs, separated
  Cream or whipped cream

Preheat oven to 325°F.

In the top of a double boiler over hot water, melt the butter and blend in the flour. Gradually add the milk and cook over hot water, stirring constantly, until thick.

Place the chocolate in a bowl over hot water and melt; add the 3 tablespoons hot water. Mix until smooth.

Add with the sugar, salt, and vanilla to the hot milk mixture. Beat the yolks and add to the milk mixture.

On a large open platter, beat the egg whites until stiff and fold in. Pour into prepared baking dish and bake for 50–60 minutes until a silver knife inserted into the soufflé comes out clean.

Serve immediately with cream or whipped cream.

Serves 4.

Soufflé for Two

5-inch baking dish, buttered

1 tablespoon butter
2 tablespoons flour
½ cup milk
1 square (1 ounce) bitter chocolate
2 tablespoons water
3–4 tablespoons sugar
¼ teaspoon vanilla
2 eggs, separated

Preheat oven to 325°F.

In a saucepan, melt the butter, whisk in the flour and the milk, then cook, stirring, until smooth.

In the top of a double boiler over hot water, melt the chocolate with the water and sugar. Add to the milk along with vanilla and cool.

Beat the egg yolks and add.

On a large open platter, beat the egg whites until stiff and fold in gently. Pour into the baking dish, set in a pan of hot water, and bake for 30–40 minutes until a silver knife inserted into the soufflé comes out clean.

Serves 2.

Mousses

The Decadent Mousse

Eat your chocolate heart out! And this recipe can be doubled.

2-quart mold, rinsed in cold water

4 squares (4 ounces) bitter chocolate
4 squares (4 ounces) sweet chocolate
½ cup plus 1 tablespoon sugar
2 egg whites, stiffly beaten
2 tablespoons plus 1 teaspoon dark rum
2 cups whipping cream, whipped
½ cup heavy cream

In the top of a double boiler over hot water, combine the two chocolates, stirring to blend. Remove from heat and cool.

Slowly beat ½ cup of the sugar into the stiffly beaten egg whites and combine with the cooled melted chocolate. Add 2 tablespoons of the rum and, lastly, fold in the whipped cream until all white streaks are gone.

Spoon into mold and refrigerate for 3 hours. To serve, unmold.

Whip the heavy cream with 1 tablespoon of sugar and 1 teaspoon of rum, and pass with the mousse.

Serves 8–10.

Variation: For variety, change the liqueur to Grand Marnier, Kahlua, curaçao, or whatever turns you on!

Italian Chocolate Mousse

My grateful thanks to Galliano International for this delicious mousse.

---

  6 champagne glasses

 12 squares (12 ounces) semisweet chocolate
  2 teaspoons instant coffee
  6 tablespoons boiling water
  4 eggs
  1 cup boiling hot milk
  ¼ cup Galliano
  1 cup whipping cream
  3 tablespoons sugar
  6 maraschino cherries

In the top of a double boiler over hot water, melt the chocolate. Remove from heat.

Dissolve the coffee in 6 tablespoons boiling water.

Beat the eggs with an electric mixer until light and lemony. Add the dissolved coffee and hot milk very slowly, beating constantly. Blend in the melted chocolate and liqueur, and beat on high for 1 minute.

Spoon into the glasses and chill.

Whip the cream with the sugar.

When the mousse is set, top with the whipped cream and garnish with cherries.

Serves 6.

Blender Mousse

This is a lifesaver when unexpected guests arrive for dinner.

---

4 dessert ramekins

6 ounces semisweet chocolate bits

2 eggs

3 tablespoons extra-strong hot coffee

2½ tablespoons rum

⅔ cup scalded milk

½ cup whipping cream

1 tablespoon sugar

Bitter chocolate, shaved

Combine the first five ingredients in a blender and blend on high for 2–3 minutes. Spoon into 4 dessert ramekins and chill for about 1 hour. Whip the cream with the sugar.

When mousse is set, garnish each serving with a dollop of whipped cream and shaved bitter chocolate.

Serves 4.

Cold Cashew Mousse

Something a bit different.

1-quart soufflé dish

2 squares (2 ounces) bitter chocolate
½ cup plus 1 tablespoon sugar
5 eggs, separated
1 cup toasted and ground cashews
1½ cups whipping cream, whipped
2 teaspoons vanilla

In the top of a double boiler over hot water, combine the chocolate and the ½ cup of sugar, and heat until melted and dissolved. Remove from heat and beat in the egg yolks, 1 at a time, beating well after each addition. Stir in the cashews and fold in gently 1 cup of the cream, whipped, with 1 teaspoon of the vanilla.

On a large open platter, whip the egg whites to a stiff peak and fold them gently into the mixture. Pour into the soufflé dish and chill for 3–4 hours.

Whip the remaining ½ cup of whipping cream with 1 tablespoon of sugar and 1 teaspoon of vanilla.

Serve the mousse with the sweetened whipped cream.
Serves 6–8.

Armagnac Mousse

A mélange of honey and chocolate. Serve with a chocolate sauce as additional garnish, if desired.

1-quart mold, rinsed with cold water

- 3 squares (3 ounces) semisweet chocolate
- 1 square (1 ounce) bitter chocolate
- ¼ cup honey
- 1½ teaspoons instant coffee
- 1½ tablespoons Armagnac
- 1 cup whipping cream, whipped

In the top of a double boiler over hot water, melt both chocolates with the honey.

Dissolve the coffee in the Armagnac and add to the chocolate mixture. Remove from heat and cool.

Fold in the whipped cream and spoon into mold.

Chill at least 4 hours.

Serves 6.

Supreme Chocolate Mousse

A blend of two luxuries—chocolate and Triple Sec. Use your prettiest mold.

1½-quart mold, rinsed with cold water

¼ cup cold milk
1 envelope unflavored gelatin
¾ cup milk, heated to boiling
7 tablespoons Triple Sec
1 egg
¼ cup plus 3 tablespoons sugar
⅛ teaspoon salt
6 ounces semisweet chocolate bits
1 cup heavy cream
2 ice cubes
1 cup whipping cream

Combine the cold milk and gelatin in a blender and beat until gelatin is softened.

Add the hot milk and blend until the gelatin is completely dissolved, then add 6 tablespoons of the liqueur, egg, ¼ cup of sugar, salt, and chocolate. Blend until the mixture is smooth.

Add the heavy cream and ice cubes and blend until the ice is melted. Turn into rinsed mold and chill until set.

Unmold. Whip the cream with 3 tablespoons of sugar and 1 tablespoon of liqueur, and serve with the mousse.

Serves 8–10.

Variation: The liqueur can be curaçao, Grand Marnier, crème de cacao, Tia Maria, or Kahlua. Use the same liqueur in the mousse and the whipped cream.

Russes and More

Macaroon Cream Cake

This is pure enchantment.

8-inch springform pan, buttered

8 squares (8 ounces) semisweet chocolate
4 tablespoons water
4 eggs, separated
1 cup confectioner's sugar
1 teaspoon vanilla
⅛ teaspoon salt
¾ pound macaroons
1 cup whipping cream, whipped
   Bitter chocolate, grated

In the top of a double boiler over hot water, melt the chocolate with the water.

Beat the egg yolks. Add the beaten yolks and sugar, and cook slowly, stirring until smooth. Cool.

Add the vanilla.

On a large open platter, beat the egg whites with the salt until stiff. Fold in the egg whites.

Line the bottom and sides of the pan with ¾ of the macaroons. Fill the mold with chocolate mixture and top with remaining macaroons. Refrigerate for several hours.

Unmold and cover top and sides with whipped cream. Garnish with grated bitter chocolate.

Serves 8–10.

Chocolate Charlotte Russe

A sophisticated classic. This is also good spiked with a little rum—dip the ladyfingers or sponge cake in the spirit. Or toss a handful of miniature marshmallows into the cooled mixture before pouring it into the mold.

1½–2-quart mold, rinsed with cold water

  2 tablespoons unflavored gelatin
  ¼ cup cold water
  2 squares (2 ounces) bitter chocolate, grated
  2 cups milk
  1 cup plus 3 tablespoons sugar
  ¾ teaspoon vanilla
  3 cups whipping cream
 18 ladyfingers, split
    or
    slices of sponge cake
    Ground nuts
    Maraschino cherries

Put the gelatin in the cold water to dissolve.

In the top of a double boiler over hot water, melt the chocolate. Add the milk and 1 cup of sugar, and cook until smooth, stirring, about 5 minutes. Combine with the gelatin mixture and stir until dissolved. When cool, add the vanilla.

Beat two cups of the whipping cream until stiff, add the melted chocolate and gelatin mixture, and stir until it thickens.

Line the bottom and sides of the mold with 13–14 ladyfingers, rounded side facing out, or the sponge cake, reserving the rest for the top. Pour the mixture into the mold and top with reserved ladyfingers or sponge cake. Refrigerate until set, about two hours.

Whip the remaining 1 cup of whipping cream with the 3 tablespoons of sugar, and the rum if desired.

Unmold the russe on a platter and garnish with the flavored whipped cream, ground nuts, and maraschino cherries.

Serves 8–10.

Frozen Orange Chocolate Charlotte

Prepared ahead of time, this dessert will keep a month in the freezer.

5-cup mold, lightly buttered

- 18 ladyfingers, split and brushed with curaçao
- 1 pound semisweet chocolate
- 2 egg yolks
- 3 tablespoons extra-strong coffee
- 3 tablespoons curaçao
- 3 egg whites, stiffly beaten
- ¾ cup whipping cream, whipped

Topping:

- 1¼ cups heavy cream
- ¼ cup confectioner's sugar
- 2 tablespoons curaçao
- Semisweet chocolate, grated

Line the bottom and sides of the mold with 12 of the ladyfingers, rounded side facing out.

In the top of a double boiler over hot water, melt the chocolate.

Beat the egg yolks with an electric mixer until light, then very slowly add the melted chocolate, coffee, and liqueur, mixing thoroughly.

Fold in the stiffly beaten egg whites and whipped cream.

Spoon the mixture into prepared mold and chill for at least two hours. Cover the top with the remaining ladyfingers, rounded side out. Seal tightly with foil and freeze.

To make the topping: Whip the heavy cream with the confectioner's sugar and add the liqueur. To serve, invert the charlotte onto a platter and cover top and sides with the flavored whipped cream. Garnish with grated chocolate.

Serves 8–10.

Macaroon Rum Charlotte

A delicate dessert and easy to prepare.

1-quart mold or 6 parfait glasses

1 tablespoon gelatin
2 tablespoons cold water
1½ squares (1½ ounces) bitter chocolate
1½ cups milk
½ cup plus 1 tablespoon sugar
⅛ teaspoon salt
½ cup whipping cream, whipped
¾ cups crushed almond macaroons
1 tablespoon dark rum
Maraschino cherries

Soak the gelatin in the cold water.

In the top of a double boiler over hot water, combine the chocolate with the milk until the chocolate is melted. Remove from heat and add the gelatin mixture with the sugar and salt. Stir until well blended. Chill until slightly thickened.

Fold the whipped cream into the mixture along with the crushed macaroons and the rum. Save some macaroon crumbs for garnish. Spoon into mold or parfait glasses and top with reserved crumbs and maraschino cherries. Chill until set.

Serves 6.

Chocolate Marshmallow Dessert

This recipe is best made the day before.

8-inch square pan

1 stick butter
½ cup confectioner's sugar, sifted
3 eggs, separated
1 small can (⅔ cup) Hershey's syrup
½ cup broken pecans
1 small package (about 4 ounces) miniature marshmallows
1½ cups whipping cream, whipped
16 graham crackers, crushed
1 tablespoon sugar

Cream together the butter and sugar, and add the egg yolks, 1 at a time. Beat well. Add the chocolate syrup, nuts, and marshmallows, and fold in 1 cup of the whipped cream.

On a large open platter, beat the egg whites until stiff and fold them in last.

Sprinkle half of the crumbs in the bottom of the pan, pour in half of the chocolate mixture, sprinkle with half of the remaining crumbs, add another layer of the chocolate mixture, and top with the remaining crumbs. Refrigerate.

Whip the ½ cup of whipping cream with 1 tablespoon of sugar. Serve this dessert with a dollop of the sweetened whipped cream.

Serves 8.

Coffee Marshmallow Cream

A delicious do-ahead dessert.

6–8 parfait glasses

1 cup extra-strong coffee
16 large marshmallows
1 cup whipping cream, whipped
Bittersweet chocolate, grated

In a saucepan, combine the coffee with the marshmallows and bring to a boil. Reduce the heat and simmer, stirring frequently, until the mixture is clear. Cool and fold in the whipped cream.

Spoon into parfait glasses and chill. Before serving, sprinkle with grated bittersweet chocolate.

Serves 6–8.

Black Russian Parfait

A very elegant dessert!

8–10 parfait or sherbet glasses
⅓ cup plus 1 tablespoon sugar
3 tablespoons hot water
2 squares (2 ounces) bitter chocolate
⅓ cup plus 1 tablespoon Kahlua
3 eggs, separated
1 cup whipping cream, whipped
¼ cup powdered sugar
Bitter chocolate, grated

In a bowl, combine the ⅓ cup of sugar with the hot water.

In the top of a double boiler over hot water, melt the chocolate and add the dissolved sugar. Add ⅓ cup of the liqueur and mix well. Remove from heat.

Beat the egg yolks until thick and lemony, and mix very slowly into the chocolate mixture.

On a large open platter, beat the egg whites until stiff, beating in 1 tablespoon of sugar, and fold gently into the chocolate mixture. Spoon into parfait glasses and chill for several hours.

Before serving, whip the cream until stiff, flavor with the powdered sugar and 1 tablespoon of Kahlua, and use to garnish each serving. Top with grated chocolate.

Serves 6–8.

Zabaglione Parfait

There is no cure for a chocoholic. Alas—he must go through life with a constant craving for chocolate! So, let's begin to satisfy.

---

6 parfait glasses

3 squares (3 ounces) semisweet chocolate
2 tablespoons light cream
¼ cup sugar
4 egg yolks
½ cup Marsala wine
½ cup whipping cream
  Bitter chocolate, grated

In the top of a double boiler over hot water, combine the chocolate with the light cream. Remove from heat when chocolate is melted. In the top of the double boiler over hot water, combine the sugar and the egg yolks, and beat until frothy. Add the Marsala wine and beat rapidly until thick. Remove from heat and beat 3–4 minutes more to cool. Add the chocolate mixture, blend well, and spoon into parfait glasses. Garnish the top with whipped cream and grated chocolate. Chill.

Serves 6.

Variation: Blend the whipped cream into the zabaglione mixture and freeze. Top with additional whipped cream and grated chocolate.

A Chocolate Mountain

Chocolate and dark rum marry well in this delightful creation.

1-quart soufflé dish

1 cup extra-fine sugar
2 tablespoons instant espresso coffee
½ cup boiling water
1 cup cocoa
5 egg yolks
¼ cup plus 2 tablespoons dark rum
5 egg whites
  Pinch salt
1 cup whipping cream
2 tablespoons confectioner's sugar
  Bittersweet chocolate, grated

In a bowl, dissolve the sugar and the coffee in the boiling water. In the top of a double boiler over simmering water, put the cocoa and slowly add the coffee mixture, stirring. Heat for about 3–5 minutes. Add the egg yolks, 1 at a time, beating well after each addition.

Remove from heat and add the ¼ cup of rum. Blend and cool.

On a large open platter, beat the egg whites with the pinch of salt until stiff and fold into the cooled mixture. Spoon into the soufflé dish and chill overnight.

Whip the cream with the remaining 2 tablespoons of rum and confectioner's sugar, and use to garnish the mousse. Dust the top with grated bittersweet chocolate and serve.

Serves 8–10.

Blender Bavarian Cream

A wonderful quick dessert for last-minute company.

1-quart dessert mold or 4–6 parfait glasses

2 envelopes unflavored gelatin
¾ cup hot water
6 ounces semisweet chocolate bits
2 tablespoons sugar
2 egg yolks
1 cup light cream
½ teaspoon vanilla
1 heaping cup crushed ice
½ cup whipping cream

In the container of an electric blender, combine the gelatin and the hot water. Cover and blend on high speed for 40 seconds.

Add the chocolate bits and 1 tablespoon of the sugar. Cover and blend another 10 seconds. With the motor on low, remove the lid and add the egg yolks, cream, vanilla, and crushed ice, only to the top of the container. Blend on medium or high. When mixture begins to thicken, turn off the motor and pour the mixture into the mold. It will be ready to serve in 5 minutes. If not to be served immediately, refrigerate.

To serve, whip the ½ cup of whipping cream with the remaining 1 tablespoon of sugar. Unmold. Garnish with whipped cream.

Serves 4–6.

Chocolate Chantilly Crème

The bitter chocolate imparts a richer flavor.

1-quart bowl for serving

1 cup sugar
½ cup water
7 squares (7 ounces) bitter chocolate
1¾ cups whipping cream
½ teaspoon vanilla

In the top of a double boiler over hot but not boiling water, dissolve the sugar in the water. Add the chocolate and melt slowly over simmering water, stirring, until all is blended. Cool.

Whip the cream to soft peaks and fold slowly into the cooled chocolate mixture with the vanilla. Beat with an electric beater until stiff. Spoon into a decorative bowl and chill.

Serves 4–6.

Venetian Pot de Crème

If you want to be different and surprise family and guests, try this crème that I had the pleasure of eating in Venice.

---

12 pot de crème pots

    1 pound ricotta cheese
 1¼ cups sugar
    5 tablespoons Aurum, if available, or curaçao
    8 squares (8 ounces) semisweet chocolate, in small pieces
  ½ cup plus 3 tablespoons water
  ¼ teaspoon cream of tartar
    4 egg yolks, beaten until light
    2 sticks sweet butter, in pieces
  ½ cup whipping cream (optional)
    1 tablespoon sugar (optional)

In a bowl, combine the ricotta, ¼ cup of sugar, 3 tablespoons of liqueur, and 2 ounces of chocolate pieces, mixing thoroughly. Spoon equally into the 12 pots. In the top of a double boiler over hot water melt the remaining 6 ounces of chocolate with 3 tablespoons of water. When melted, cool.

Make a syrup by combining the remaining 1 cup of sugar with the remaining ½ cup of water and cream of tartar in a saucepan. Boil the syrup until the temperature on a candy thermometer reaches 236°F—the soft-ball stage.

Pour the syrup in a thin stream over the beaten egg yolks and continue to beat until cool, while adding the butter. Add the melted chocolate and the remaining 2 tablespoons of liqueur. Spoon this mixture into the 12 pots over the cheese mixture and chill the pots for 3–4 hours.

No garnish is necessary, but you may whip the cream with 1 tablespoon of the sugar to add a dollop of whipped cream for a more festive look.

Serves 12.

Baked Pot de Crème

Something a little bit different.

---

8 pot de crème pots or ramekins

10 squares (10 ounces) semisweet chocolate
½ cup plus 1 tablespoon sugar
¼ cup water
 8 egg yolks, beaten lightly
 4 cups milk, scalded
½ cup whipping cream
   Semisweet chocolate, grated

Preheat oven to 325°F.

In a heavy saucepan over low heat, melt the 10 ounces of chocolate with the ½ cup of sugar and water. Pour the cooled chocolate over the beaten egg yolks slowly, beating constantly. Add the scalded milk in a steady stream, stirring until blended. Remove the froth on top, pour into the 8 pots, and cover with lids or foil. Place in a baking pan and add enough hot water to go three-fourths of the way up the sides of the pots. Bake in preheated oven for 25–30 minutes, until set.

Uncover the pots and allow to cool.

Chill before serving.

Whip the cream with 1 tablespoon of sugar. To garnish, top with whipped cream and grated semisweet chocolate.

Serves 8.

Chocolate Orange Sponge

One taste is worth a thousand pictures.

1½-quart mold, rinsed with cold water

4 eggs, separated
⅔ cup plus 3 tablespoons sugar
1 tablespoon unflavored gelatin
¼ cup cold water
1 cup boiling water
8 squares (8 ounces) bitter chocolate
⅛ teaspoon salt
1 tablespoon plus additional Grand Marnier to taste
1 cup whipping cream
  Orange zest

In a bowl, combine the egg yolks with ⅔ cup of the sugar. Beat until thick and lemony.

Soften the gelatin in the cold water, then dissolve in ½ cup of the boiling water.

In the top of a double boiler over hot water, dissolve the chocolate in the remaining ½ cup of boiling water. Add the melted chocolate to the egg mixture with the salt and 1 tablespoon of the Grand Marnier, beating well. Add the gelatin slowly, beating constantly.

On a large open platter, beat the egg whites until stiff, then fold into the chocolate mixture gently but thoroughly.

Spoon the mixture into the rinsed mold and chill in the refrigerator until firm.

Whip the cream with the remaining 3 tablespoons of sugar and Grand Marnier to taste (begin with 1 teaspoon). To serve, unmold. Garnish with whipped cream and sprinkle with orange zest.

Serves 8–10.

Ladyfinger Cake

You may use sponge cake or angel food cake instead of the ladyfingers.

        9-inch springform pan

2½ dozen ladyfingers, split
  4 eggs, separated
  8 squares (8 ounces) dark sweet chocolate
  3 tablespoons water
  4 tablespoons sugar
  ½ teaspoon vanilla
    Pinch salt
  1 cup heavy cream
  1 tablespoon Kahlua
    Maraschino cherries
    Ground nuts

Line the bottom and sides of the pan with ladyfingers, rounded side facing out.

Beat the egg yolks until light and lemony.

In the top of a double boiler over hot water, melt the chocolate with the water and 3 tablespoons of the sugar. Add the beaten yolks very slowly; cook, stirring constantly, until thick. Cool and add the vanilla.

On a large open platter, beat the egg whites with pinch salt until stiff. Fold into mixture.

Pour ½ of the mixture into the lined pan—one layer of filling, a layer of ladyfingers, and so on until all is used (2 layers filling, 3 layers ladyfingers). The top layer should be cake. Chill until set, about 8 hours.

Remove from pan. Whip the cream with the remaining 1 tablespoon of sugar and Kahlua. Cover the cake with the flavored whipped cream and garnish with cherries or nuts or both.

Serves 10–12.

PUDDINGS

Bride's Chocolate Pudding
Kahlua Chocolate Velvet
Chocolate Date-Nut Pudding
Chocolate Rice Pudding
Chocolate Blancmange
Macaroon Pudding with Sweet Chocolate
French Custard
Baked Mocha Custard
Upside-Down Pudding
Chocolate Bread Pudding
Chocolate Cottage Pudding

Bride's Chocolate Pudding

Foolproof enough for a novice.

---

6 sherbet glasses

1½ cups plus 1 tablespoon sugar
3 squares (3 ounces) bitter chocolate
½ teaspoon salt
3 tablespoons flour
3 cups milk
3 egg yolks
1 tablespoon butter
1½ teaspoons vanilla
1 tablespoon plus additional Tia Maria to taste
½ cup whipping cream

In a saucepan, combine 1½ cups of the sugar, chocolate, salt, and flour. Gradually stir in the milk. Cook over medium heat, stirring constantly, until the mixture thickens and boils. Boil 1 minute and remove from heat.

Beat the egg yolks. Stir ½ of the chocolate mixture very slowly into the yolks. Blend in the rest of the chocolate mixture and cook 1 minute more with yolks, over low heat, stirring to cook yolks. Remove from heat. Add the butter, vanilla, and 1 tablespoon of the liqueur. Pour into sherbet glasses and chill.

Whip the cream with 1 tablespoon of the sugar and Tia Maria to taste (begin with 1 teaspoon). Top each serving with flavored whipped cream.

Serves 6.

Kahlua Chocolate Velvet

The incomparable Kahlua kitchen has done it again!

1-quart serving bowl

⅓ cup Kahlua
½ teaspoon instant coffee
½ teaspoon vanilla
2 squares (2 ounces) bitter chocolate
4 squares (4 ounces) semisweet chocolate
5 eggs, separated
¼ teaspoon cream of tartar
⅓ cup extra-fine sugar

In the top of a double boiler over hot water, combine the liqueur, coffee, vanilla, and chocolates. Stir frequently until the mixture is melted and smooth.

Beat the egg yolks in the bowl of an electric mixer until light, then add the chocolate mixture. Blend and cool.

On a large open platter, beat the egg whites with the cream of tartar to soft peaks, then gradually beat in the sugar until stiff.

Beat half of the meringue into the chocolate mixture until smooth, then fold in the remaining meringue. Turn into the serving bowl, cover, and chill until firm.

Serves 8.

Chocolate Date-Nut Pudding

Sheer goodness!

9-inch square pan, buttered

½ cup sugar
3 tablespoons butter or shortening
2½ squares (2½ ounces) bitter chocolate
1½ cups flour, sifted
1½ teaspoons baking powder
½ teaspoon cinnamon
  Pinch salt
¾ cup milk
1 cup chopped pitted dates
½ cup chopped walnuts
½ teaspoon vanilla
½ teaspoon grated orange rind
2 cups boiling water
1 cup packed brown sugar
  Ice cream, any flavor

Preheat oven to 350°F.

In a bowl, cream together the sugar and 1 tablespoon of the butter or shortening until well blended.

In the top of a double boiler over hot water melt the chocolate. Add to the butter mixture.

Resift the flour with the baking powder, cinnamon, and salt. Add to the butter mixture alternately with the milk. Add the dates and nuts, and mix well. Add the vanilla and orange rind.

Combine the boiling water, brown sugar, and remaining 2 tablespoons of butter or shortening in a saucepan and bring to the boiling point.

Spread the chocolate batter evenly into the pan, then pour the brown sugar mixture over the batter. Bake in preheated oven for 45 minutes until set.

Serve warm with ice cream.

Serves 6–8.

Chocolate Rice Pudding

An old-timer dressed up.

---

    4 cups milk
    ½ cup uncooked rice
    ¼ teaspoon salt
    5 tablespoons sugar plus additional to taste
    1 tablespoon butter
    1 tablespoon bitter chocolate, grated
    1 teaspoon vanilla
    ½ cup whipping cream, whipped

In the top of a double boiler over hot water, heat the milk, then add the rice, salt, sugar, butter, chocolate, and vanilla. Add more sugar, if needed, to taste. Cover and cook over low heat for 2 hours.

Serve chilled or at room temperature with lightly sweetened whipped cream.

Serves 6–8.

Chocolate Blancmange

Very traditional.

1-quart mold, rinsed in cold water

1 tablespoon gelatin
2 tablespoons cold water
1¾ cups milk
2½ squares (2½ ounces) bitter chocolate, broken into pieces
½ cup plus 5 tablespoons sugar
¼ teaspoon salt
1¾ teaspoons vanilla
2 cups whipping cream
3 tablespoons sugar
1 tablespoon rum, sherry, or vanilla

Dissolve the gelatin in the cold water.

In a saucepan, scald the milk and add the chocolate, ½ cup and 2 tablespoons of sugar, and salt. Stir until the chocolate and sugar are dissolved. Add the gelatin mixture and chill until thickened.

When thickened, add the vanilla.

Whip 1 cup of the whipping cream until stiff and fold into the mixture. Pour into the mold and chill thoroughly.

To serve, whip the remaining cup of cream with 3 tablespoons of the sugar and flavoring. Unmold the pudding onto a platter and serve with the flavored whipped cream.

Serves 8–10.

Variation: This may be poured into an 8-inch springform pan or loaf pan lined with macaroons, ladyfingers, or cake slices.

Macaroon Pudding with Sweet Chocolate

This is as rich as Croesus!

1-quart mold, rinsed with cold water

 1 tablespoon gelatin
 2 tablespoons cold water
 ¼ cup boiling water
2½ cups whipping cream
 4 squares (4 ounces) dark sweet chocolate
 ½ teaspoon vanilla
 8 macaroons, crushed
 1 tablespoon rum
 1 tablespoon sugar
    Maraschino cherries

Combine the gelatin with the cold water to dissolve, then add the boiling water and stir. Chill.

Whip 2 cups of the cream.

When the gelatin mix is cold, add to the cream. Divide this mixture into two parts. To one half, add the grated chocolate and vanilla; to the other, add the crumbled macaroons and rum.

Place the mixture in the mold in alternate layers. Refrigerate for 1–2 hours. Unmold. Whip the remaining cream with the sugar and serve with the mold. Garnish with maraschino cherries.

Serves 6–8.

French Custard

Definitely one of the best.

1-quart baking pan or 10–12 custard cups

1⅓ cups milk
1⅓ cups light cream
  6 squares (6 ounces) dark sweet chocolate
  6 eggs
    Pinch salt
1¼ teaspoons vanilla
  1 cup whipping cream
  5 tablespoons sugar

Preheat oven to 325°F.

In the top of a double boiler over simmering water, combine the milk, cream, 4 tablespoons of sugar, and chocolate and simmer until the chocolate is melted and the milk is hot. Stir frequently. Remove from heat.

Beat the eggs until light and lemony, and very slowly blend into the chocolate mixture. Add the salt and vanilla, and strain into the baking dish or individual custard cups. Set in a pan of hot water and bake in oven for 50–60 minutes, until a silver knife inserted into the center comes out clean. Chill.

Whip the cream with the remaining sugar and serve with the custard.

Serves 8–10.

Baked Mocha Custard

1-quart baking dish or 6 individual molds

½ cup grated bitter chocolate
1 cup strong coffee
½ cup light cream
½ cup milk
7–8 tablespoons sugar
Pinch salt
2 eggs
1 tablespoon Kahlua
1 cup whipping cream

Preheat oven to 325°F.

In the top of a double boiler over simmering water, combine the chocolate, coffee, light cream, milk, 5–6 tablespoons of sugar, and salt. Cook only to the boiling point—do not allow to boil—and stir constantly. Remove from heat.

Beat the eggs and pour the chocolate mixture slowly over the eggs, beating until well blended. Pour into the baking dish or individual molds and place in a pan of hot water in preheated oven. Bake for about 1 hour, until a silver knife inserted into the center comes out clean.

Whip the cream with the remaining 2 tablespoons of sugar and Kahlua, and serve with the custard.

Serves 6.

Upside-Down Pudding

Easy and different.

1½-quart shallow baking dish, buttered

1½ squares (1½ ounces) bitter chocolate
2 tablespoons butter
1 egg
½ cup milk
1¼ teaspoon vanilla
1¼ cups cake flour, sifted
1 cup plus 7 tablespoons sugar
¼ teaspoon salt
1½ teaspoons baking powder
⅓ cup chopped pecans or almonds
2 tablespoons cocoa
½ cup dark brown sugar, packed
1 cup boiling water
½ cup light cream, whipping cream, or ice cream
2 teaspoons rum

Preheat oven to 350°F.

In the top of a double boiler over simmering water, combine the chocolate and butter until melted. Cool slightly.

Beat the egg until light. Add the milk and vanilla. Blend the milk mixture into the chocolate mixture.

Resift the flour with ¾ cup and 2 tablespoons of sugar, salt, and baking powder, 3 times. Pour the chocolate mixture into the dry ingredients and stir until mixed. Add the nuts and pour into prepared baking dish.

Combine the cocoa with ½ cup of the sugar and the brown sugar, and sprinkle over the top of the pudding. Pour the boiling water over all and bake in oven for 45–55 minutes, until a silver knife inserted in the center comes out clean.

Blend the light cream with the remaining 1 tablespoon of sugar and rum. If using whipped cream, whip the cream with the sugar and rum.

Serve warm with light cream, whipped cream, or ice cream.

Serves 6–8.

Chocolate Bread Pudding

An old classic in a new dress.

1-quart baking dish, buttered

2 cups milk
¾ cup bread crumbs
1 square (1 ounce) bitter chocolate
½ cup sugar
¾ teaspoon vanilla
Pinch salt
1 egg, beaten
Light cream

Preheat oven to 350°F.

Scald 1½ cups of the milk and stir in the bread crumbs. Allow to stand for about 20 minutes.

Meanwhile, in the top of a double boiler over hot but not boiling water, melt the chocolate and add the sugar and the remaining ½ cup of milk. Stir until smooth.

Remove from heat and add to the bread mixture with the salt, vanilla, and beaten egg. Blend well and spoon into prepared baking dish.

Bake in preheated oven for about 30 minutes or until set.

Serve warm and pass a pitcher of cream.

Serves 4–5.

Chocolate Cottage Pudding

Another old-fashioned dessert; updated. Serve this with a fudge sauce or chocolate sauce (see pp. 182–190).

8-inch square pan, buttered

¼ cup shortening
¾ cup sugar
2 eggs
2¼ cups flour
¼ teaspoon salt
3 teaspoons baking powder
¾ cup milk
½ cup chopped semisweet chocolate, grated

Preheat oven to 375°F.

In a bowl, cream together the shortening and the sugar.

Add the eggs, 1 at a time, beating well after each addition.

Sift together the flour, salt, and baking powder. Add alternately with the milk to the sugar mixture. Add the chocolate.

Pour into prepared pan. Bake for 40 minutes, until a silver knife inserted into the center comes out clean. Serve hot with any fudge or chocolate sauce.

Serves 6.

ICE CREAMS

Ice Cream Pies
Super Sundaes
Never-Fail Chocolate Ice Cream
Fluffy Chocolate Cream
Triple Sec Chocolate Ice Cream
Chocolate Hazelnut Ice Cream
Chocolate Mallow Ice Cream
Frozen Chocolate Cream
Quick Ice Cream
Mocha Ice Cream
Chocolate Mocha Cream Whip
Chocolate Chip Ice Cream Loaf
Orange Bombe
Frozen Framboise Bombe

Ice Cream Pies

As easy as they are delicious, ice cream pies are great any time of year.

Soften the ice cream, put in a pie shell, and freeze. Fill an 8-inch pie with 2 pints of ice cream, a 9-inch pie with 3 pints. Pie shells should be chocolate crumb or chocolate pastry shells, baked and cooled.

Suggested ice cream combinations: chocolate ice cream topped with pistachio ice cream, strawberry ice cream with orange ice, cherry-vanilla ice cream with pineapple ice, strawberry ice cream with lemon ice blended with diced glazed fruits.

Variation: Liqueur can be blended into softened ice cream *or* blended into whipped cream to top the pie. Then freeze.

Ice Cream Pie Shell:
Baked pie shell, cooled.
Melt your favorite chocolate bar and cover the bottom and sides. Refrigerate until ready to fill. The chocolate coating will prevent the crust from becoming soft and will certainly enhance the flavor of the dessert. For Chocolate Crumb Crust recipe, see page 62.

Super Sundaes

Great last-minute desserts

Per serving:
Over chocolate ice cream, pour 1 tablespoon Kahlua.
Over chocolate ice cream, pour 1 tablespoon any orange liqueur.
Over chocolate or chocolate chip ice cream, pour 1 tablespoon Amaretto.
Over vanilla or coffee ice cream, pour 1 tablespoon crème de cacao.
Over banana ice cream, pour 1 tablespoon crème de cacao.

Never-Fail Chocolate Ice Cream

1 square (1 ounce) bitter chocolate, grated
1 teaspoon gelatin
⅓ cup sugar
1 tablespoon flour
Pinch salt
1 cup milk
2 eggs, separated
¼ cup light corn syrup
2 teaspoons vanilla
1 cup whipping cream

In a saucepan, mix together the chocolate, gelatin, sugar, flour, and salt. Stir in the milk and the egg yolks. Cook over medium heat, beating constantly, until thickened. Chill.

On a large open platter, beat the egg whites until stiff but not dry. Beat in the corn syrup gradually; add the vanilla and beat until well blended. Add to custard mixture and mix well.

Whip the cream and fold in. Pour into an ice cream freezer and follow manufacturer's directions.

Makes 1 quart.

Fluffy Chocolate Cream

Frozen paradise.

4½ squares (4½ ounces) bitter chocolate
 4 eggs, separated
1½ cups sugar
 2 cups evaporated milk
 2 cups milk
2½ teaspoons vanilla
 ¼ teaspoon salt

In the top of a double boiler over simmering water, melt the chocolate.

Beat egg yolks until light and lemony, gradually adding the sugar.

Add the melted chocolate slowly, stirring constantly until well blended.

In a saucepan, combine both milks and scald. Pour a little of the scalded milk over the chocolate mixture, beating well, then add it all, beating. Chill the custard, then add the vanilla. Pour into refrigerator trays and freeze until just firm.

On a large open platter, beat the egg whites with the salt until stiff peaks are formed. Remove the custard from the trays into a bowl. Mix, fold in the whites, return to trays, and *freeze* again.

Makes 2 quarts.

Triple Sec Chocolate Ice Cream

Every chocolate lover's dream—chocolate with orange.

2½ squares (2½ ounces) bitter chocolate
1 cup sugar
3 egg yolks, beaten
¼ teaspoon salt
2 cups milk, heated
¼ cup Triple Sec
1 tablespoon grated orange zest
2 cups whipping cream, whipped

In a heavy saucepan, melt the chocolate over low heat.

Mix in the sugar, beaten egg yolks, and salt, stirring constantly until well blended.

Add the hot milk very gradually while continuing to stir constantly and cook over moderate heat about 3–5 minutes, stirring until smooth.

Remove from heat and add the Triple Sec and the zest. Allow to cool.

Fold in the whipped cream. Pour into an electric ice cream freezer and freeze according to manufacturer's directions.

Makes about 3 quarts.

Chocolate Hazelnut Ice Cream

Who could resist this combination!

---

    2   cups hazelnuts
   12   squares (12 ounces) semisweet chocolate bits
    1   square (1 ounce) bitter chocolate
   ⅓   cup water
    4   teaspoons instant espresso coffee
    4   teaspoons hot water
    2   cups heavy cream, scalded
    8   egg yolks
    1   cup extra-fine sugar

Spread the hazelnuts on a cookie sheet and roast at 350°F for 10–15 minutes, until the skins are loose. Wrap them in a towel and let them steam until the skins can be rubbed off, about 1 minute. Chop and reserve.

In a saucepan, combine both chocolates with the water and cook over low heat, stirring until smooth and melted.

In a bowl, dissolve the espresso in the hot water and add the scalded heavy cream.

In a separate bowl, beat the egg yolks and the sugar with an electric beater until a ribbon forms when the beater is lifted, then add the chocolate mixture and the cream mixture, beating well.

Pour the custard into a saucepan and cook over low heat until it is thickened and coats a spoon. Do not boil.

Transfer the custard to a bowl set over ice and stir until cold.

Pour the mixture into an electric ice cream freezer and freeze 10 minutes. Add nuts and freeze according to manufacturer's instructions.

Makes 2½ quarts.

Chocolate Mallow Ice Cream

1½ cups evaporated milk
2 squares (2 ounces) bitter chocolate
6 tablespoons sugar
¼ teaspoon salt
½ cup water
4 ounces marshmallows

Thoroughly chill 1 cup of the evaporated milk.

In the top of a double boiler, combine the chocolate, sugar, and salt with the remaining milk and water. Cook over simmering water until smooth. Add the marshmallows and stir until melted.

Whip the cold evaporated milk until stiff and fold into the cooled mixture. Freeze in refrigerator trays until hard.

Makes 1½ pints.

Frozen Chocolate Cream

Serve with your favorite sauce.

2 squares (2 ounces) bitter chocolate
2 cups heavy cream
½ cup confectioner's sugar
   Pinch salt
1 teaspoon vanilla

In the top of a double boiler, add the chocolate to ½ cup of the cream and heat over hot water until melted. Add the sugar and salt, and mix well. Whip the remaining cream slightly and add with the vanilla to the chocolate mixture. Pour into freezer trays and freeze until firm.

Serves 8.

Quick Ice Cream

1 square (1 ounce) bitter chocolate
⅔ cup sweetened condensed milk
⅔ cup water
   Pinch salt
⅔ cup whipping cream
1 teaspoon vanilla

In the top of a double boiler over simmering water, melt the chocolate. Add the milk. Cook, stirring constantly, for 5 minutes, until thick. Gradually add the water and salt. Chill.

Whip the cream slightly; fold into the chocolate mixture with the vanilla and pour into freezer trays. Freeze to mush.

Place in a chilled bowl and beat until smooth, then return to trays and freeze until hard.

Serves 4–6.

Variation: For an unusual flavor, reduce the vanilla to ¼ teaspoon and add ½ teaspoon of cinnamon. Keeps the folks guessing!

Mocha Ice Cream

All the world loves a lover—especially a chocolate lover!

1½ cups light cream
½ cup sugar
2½ squares (2½ ounces) bitter chocolate
2 tablespoons instant coffee
Pinch salt
4 egg yolks
2 cups heavy cream
⅓ cup semisweet chocolate bits

In the top of a double boiler over hot water, scald the light cream. Add the sugar, bitter chocolate, coffee, and salt, and blend until the chocolate is melted.

Beat the egg yolks and very slowly add them to the chocolate-cream mixture, stirring constantly, until thickened. Remove from heat and cool.

Blend in the heavy cream and chocolate bits, and spoon into an electric freezer. Freeze according to manufacturer's instructions.

Makes 1 quart.

Chocolate Mocha Cream Whip

1 teaspoon cornstarch
1 cup sugar
1 cup strong hot coffee
4 eggs, separated
8 squares (8 ounces) dark sweet chocolate
Pinch salt
2 cups whipping cream
1 teaspoon vanilla

Combine cornstarch, sugar, and coffee. Beat the egg yolks until light and, stirring constantly, gradually pour into the coffee mixture.

In the top of a double boiler, melt the chocolate and add the coffee mixture. Cook, stirring, until smooth.

On a large open platter, beat the egg whites with a pinch of salt. Whip the cream with the vanilla.

When the coffee mixture is cool, fold in the egg whites and the whipped cream. Pour into an electric freezer and freeze according to manufacturer's instructions.

Makes 1½ quarts.

Chocolate Chip Ice Cream Loaf

Every freezer should have one ready for any occasion.

---

10 × 4-inch loaf pan, lined with wax paper

12 ladyfingers, split
1 quart chocolate chip ice cream
1 cup crushed almond macaroons
2 tablespoons dark rum

Line the bottom and sides of the loaf pan with ladyfingers, rounded side out. Reserve remaining ladyfingers.

Soften the ice cream and blend with crushed macaroons and rum.

Spoon the mixture into the prepared loaf pan, top with reserved ladyfingers, cover tightly with foil, and freeze for 2–3 hours.

To serve, run knife around edge of pan and unmold and serve with Chocolate Cream Sauce (see page 186).

Serves 8–10.

Orange Bombe

A fun and easy dessert to prepare and serve.

Quart mold, chilled

1 quart coffee or chocolate ice cream
1 pint orange sherbet

Press slightly softened ice cream on the bottom and sides of the mold, and freeze. Fill the hollow with orange sherbet and freeze until ready to serve.

To unmold, dip the mold in cool water for about 5 seconds, then invert on a chilled serving dish.

Slice and serve with semisweet chocolate sauce lightly flavored with curaçao.

Serves 6–8.

Frozen Framboise Bombe

An absolute joy to prepare and serve, sent to me by my cousin Beatrice Kolliner.

2-quart mold, rinsed with cold water

1¾ cups crushed almond macaroons
2½ tablespoons Kirsch
1 cup whipping cream
3½ tablespoons framboise liqueur—use only the red
1 quart rich vanilla ice cream, softened
1 cup chopped and toasted blanched almonds
⅔ cup coarsely grated semisweet chocolate
Fresh raspberries

Blend the crushed macaroons with the Kirsch and allow to stand while preparing the rest of the bombe.

In the large chilled bowl of an electric mixer, beat the cream until fluffy and quickly fold in remaining ingredients except raspberries. Blend well, spoon into the mold, and freeze until firm.

To unmold, wrap a hot wet towel over the bottom of the mold.

Serve with fresh raspberries when in season.

Serves 8–10.

FRUIT

Poires Hélène
Chocolate Orange Slices
Stuffed Chocolate Dates
Chocolate-dipped Orange Peel
Strawberry Paradise
Fruit Laced with Liqueur

Poires Hélène

A classic dessert that is welcome summer and winter.

½ teaspoon vanilla
6 canned pear halves, drained
1 quart vanilla ice cream
Hot fudge sauce

In a saucepan, combine the vanilla with the juice from the canned pears. Cook slowly about 5 minutes. Remove from heat, place the pears in the syrup, and allow to cool. Then chill.

To serve, spoon the ice cream onto 6 chilled dessert plates, place a pear half on each, rounded side up, and top with the hot fudge sauce.

Serves 6.

Chocolate Orange Slices

During my trip through Switzerland with my daughter Debbie, we found that many of the better candy stores along the arcade to the famous Berne Bear Pit sold fresh orange slices dipped in bittersweet chocolate. They are heavenly and easy to make. We nibbled these nearly every day of our stay.

---

4 navel oranges, peeled, sectioned, and all membranes removed
8 squares (8 ounces) bittersweet chocolate
4 tablespoons butter
¼ cup water

Place the orange sections on paper towels and let stand to dry for about 1 hour.

In the top of a double boiler over hot water, melt the chocolate with butter and water. When well blended, remove from heat.

Using a fork, dip each orange section completely into the chocolate and place on oiled wax paper. Let chocolate and orange set for at least 1 hour.

Sufficient for 4.

Variation: To serve as a dessert, arrange four orange slices on a dessert plate, sprinkle each with a teaspoon of the orange liqueur of your choice, and pass a bowl of lightly sweetened whipped cream. Ambrosial!

Stuffed Chocolate Dates

A welcome addition to a tea table, but do make these when the humidity factor is low.

½ cup ground nutmeats, pecans or walnuts
½ cup confectioner's sugar
2 tablespoons rum
7¼ ounces pitted dates

Glaze:
6 ounces semisweet chocolate bits
1 tablespoon butter
3 tablespoons light corn syrup
4 tablespoons milk

Mix the ground nuts, sugar, and rum together.

Make a slit in each date and stuff with the nut mixture.

To make the glaze: In the top of a double boiler over hot water, melt the chocolate, then stir in the butter, corn syrup, and milk, stirring until smooth. Remove the glaze from the heat. Dip both ends of the dates into the glaze. Place on rack to cool and dry, then place each stuffed date in a fluted bonbon candy cup.

Makes about ½ pound.

Chocolate-dipped Orange Peel

These are positively addictive! And grapefruit is also habit-forming.

---

    6 thick-skinned oranges
      Water
    1 teaspoon salt
    2 cups sugar
    1 cup water
    ½ cup light corn syrup
  4–6 squares (4–6 ounces) bittersweet chocolate

Preheat oven to 150°F.

Wash and dry the oranges, cut them into quarters, and remove the pulp and white pith. Place the peel in a saucepan, cover with water, add salt, and boil slowly for about 20 minutes, or until peel is tender. Drain.

Cut into ¼-inch strips. Place the sugar, corn syrup, and 1 cup of water in a saucepan and cook over medium heat, stirring constantly, until the sugar is dissolved. Add the orange peel, bring to a rapid boil, reduce heat to a slow boil, and cook uncovered for about 45 minutes, until the peel has absorbed almost all the syrup. Drain on paper towels.

Sprinkle sugar on a large sheet of wax paper and toss the peel to coat, then place on a cookie sheet and put in preheated oven for 1 hour to dry. Remove from oven and let cool on a rack for about 3 hours.

Melt sufficient chocolate in the top of a double boiler over simmering water and coat the candied peel. Let dry on wax paper.

Yield varies according to size of fruit.

Strawberry Paradise

A delightfully different dessert—quick and easy!

2-quart baking dish, buttered

2 pints strawberries, rinsed and stemmed
2–3 tablespoons orange juice
3 tablespoons curaçao, Triple Sec, or Grand Marnier
4 tablespoons dark brown sugar
1½ cups chocolate cookie crumbs
4 tablespoons butter, melted
1 cup whipping cream
3 tablespoons sugar

Preheat oven to 350°F.

Place the berries in the prepared baking dish and douse with juice and 2 tablespoons of the liqueur.

Mix the brown sugar with the crumbs and sprinkle over the berries to cover.

Spoon the melted butter over all and bake in preheated oven for 15–20 minutes. Remove from oven and serve just warm.

Whip the cream with the sugar and 1 tablespoon of liqueur and pass while serving.

Serves 6.

Variations: Fresh peaches with rum instead of the liqueur; fresh pineapple with rum; or fresh raspberries with framboise.

Fruit Laced with Liqueur

Suggested fruit-liqueur combinations:

Apples, cooked—	Calvados, apricot, Southern Comfort
Apricots, canned—	Cointreau, Triple Sec, Grand Marnier, curaçao
Bananas, baked—	Rum, apricot, Grand Marnier, Cointreau
Blueberries—	Apricot, Framboise, Triple Sec, Cointreau
Cherries, preferably bing—	Apricot, Cherry Heering, or any orange liqueur
Figs, stewed or canned—	Apricot or any orange liqueur
Oranges, sliced—	Any orange liqueur, apricot
Peaches, fresh or canned—	Rum, peach, apricot, Cassis, Framboise, or any orange liqueur
Pears, canned—	Cassis, Cherry Heering, apricot, Cointreau
Pineapple, fresh or canned—	Apricot, Cassis, Grand Marnier, Triple Sec, curaçao
Raspberries—	Cherry Heering, Cassis, Grand Marnier, Framboise
Strawberries—	Cassis, Framboise, Grand Marnier, Cointreau, Triple Sec

To use as toppings over, for example, pancakes or ice cream, marinate the fruit in liqueur or spoon liqueur over fruit. Try mashing or mincing fruit and then blend with whipped cream and liqueur. This may be topped with chocolate sauce or grated chocolate.

Amount of liqueur depends on individual taste.

SAUCES

Quick Chocolate Sauces for Ice Creams and Puddings

Hot Chocolate Sauce

Chocolate Banana Topping

The Simplest Ever Ice Cream Sauce

Lazy Day Chocolate Sauce

Quick Cognac Sauce

Chocolate Cream Sauce

Orange Chocolate Sauce

Rum Praline Sauce

Flambéed Dessert Sauce

Brandied Mint Sauce

Whipped Cream with Suggested Liqueurs

Chocolate Whipped Cream

Mexican Chocolate Sauce

Toasted Coconut

Quick Chocolate Sauces for Ice Creams and Puddings

Thin Sauce:

4 squares (4 ounces) sweet chocolate

⅔ cup water

⅓ cup sugar

2 tablespoons butter

In a saucepan, melt the chocolate and the water over low heat and stir until smooth.

Add the sugar and stir until dissolved, then boil just 4 minutes.

Remove from heat and add the butter. Stir until melted.

Serve hot.

Makes about 1 cup.

Thick Sauce:

4 squares (4 ounces) sweet chocolate

1 tablespoon water

2 tablespoons butter

In the top of a double boiler over simmering water, heat the chocolate and the water, and stir until smooth. Remove from heat and add the butter. Stir until melted.

Makes about ¾ cup.

Medium Sauce:

4 squares (4 ounces) sweet chocolate

6 tablespoons water

¼ cup sugar

2 tablespoons butter

In a saucepan, melt the chocolate and the water over low heat and stir until smooth.

Add the sugar and stir until dissolved, then boil just 4 minutes.

Remove from heat and add the butter. Stir until melted.

Serve hot.

Makes about ½ cup.

Hot Chocolate Sauce

Keep this sauce hot in the top of a double boiler and serve over any dessert pancake, vanilla custard, ice cream, or plain cake.

1½ cups sugar
4 squares (4 ounces) bitter chocolate
3 tablespoons butter
1 cup heavy cream
½ cup dry sherry
1 teaspoon vanilla

In a saucepan, combine the sugar, chocolate, butter, and cream, and stir over low heat until completely dissolved. Bring to a boil, and boil, stirring constantly, for about 5 minutes.

Remove from heat and add the sherry and vanilla. Keep warm in the top of double boiler over hot but not boiling water until ready to serve.

Makes about 2 cups.

Chocolate Banana Topping

I like to serve this sauce over coffee or vanilla ice cream.

6 squares (6 ounces) semisweet chocolate
3 tablespoons rum
⅓ cup heavy cream
1 tablespoon butter
3 small bananas, peeled and sliced
1 quart coffee or vanilla ice cream

Melt the chocolate with the rum, cream, and butter. Add the sliced bananas and warm through.

Serve in dessert dishes over the ice cream.

Serves 4.

The Simplest Ever Ice Cream Sauce

This sauce will lend a certain finesse to any ice cream, pound cake, or cream puff. Serve hot or cool.

---

    6 ounces semisweet chocolate bits
    1 teaspoon instant coffee
    6 tablespoons water
1½ tablespoons dark rum

In the top of a double boiler over hot water, melt the chocolate and the coffee in the water, stirring until smooth.

Remove from heat and add the rum to taste.

Makes about 1½ cups.

Variation: Omit the coffee and rum, and flavor with any liqueur of your choice.

Lazy Day Chocolate Sauce

Good over puddings and ice cream, and as a cake filling or a base for chocolate milk.

---

4 squares (4 ounces) bitter chocolate
¾ cup hot water, milk, cream, or evaporated milk
1 teaspoon vanilla or ½ teaspoon almond extract or ½
    teaspoon cinnamon
Pinch salt
1 cup sugar

Place all ingredients in an electric blender and blend at high speed for about 1 minute.

Makes 1½ cups.

Quick Cognac Sauce

The cook's life has been made so much easier since I was a bride. All I had then was a Mixmaster! Today we have blenders and Cuisinarts to do our time-consuming chores. I do own a blender, my one concession to kitchen magic. This sauce, made in a blender, has saved the day and a dull dessert many times.

4½ squares (4½ ounces) bittersweet chocolate, diced
1 cup sugar
1¼ teaspoons vanilla
Pinch salt
⅓ cup extra-strong coffee
⅓ cup brandy

Put the chocolate, sugar, vanilla, and salt into a blender.

In a saucepan, bring the coffee and cognac to a boil. Add to the ingredients in the blender. Cover and turn blender on for 20–30 seconds, until well blended.

Delicious over ice cream, molds, or just plain pound cake.

Makes 1½ cups.

Chocolate Cream Sauce

Devilishly delicious!

---

    1 cup sugar
    1 cup water
    ½ cup light corn syrup
    4 squares (4 ounces) bitter chocolate
    ½ cup light cream
    1 teaspoon dark rum
    1 teaspoon vanilla

In a saucepan, combine the sugar, water, and corn syrup, and bring to a boil over medium heat, stirring constantly. Continue to boil the syrup, without stirring, until the temperature on a candy thermometer reaches 236°F.

Remove from heat and add the chocolate, stirring until melted. Slowly add the cream, stirring, then add the flavorings and blend well.
Makes 2 cups.

Orange Chocolate Sauce

A honey of a topping for stewed fruit, plain cake, or ice cream.

---

    1 stick butter, melted
    ½ cup cocoa
    2 tablespoons cornstarch
    1 cup honey
    ⅔ cup water
      Pinch salt
    2 tablespoons curaçao

In a saucepan, blend together the butter, cocoa, and cornstarch. Add the honey, water, and salt, and cook over high heat, stirring constantly, until sauce is thick.

Remove from heat and flavor with the liqueur.

Serve at room temperature.
Makes 2 cups.

Rum Praline Sauce

A delicious topping for ice cream.

---

8 squares (8 ounces) milk chocolate, broken into pieces
1 cup light cream
½ cup crushed praline candy (or use 1 recipe of
    Homemade Praline, below)
2 teaspoons rum

In a saucepan, combine the chocolate and cream, and bring to a boil. Lower heat and simmer until the sauce is thick. Fold in the praline candy and rum. Serve warm.

Makes 2 cups.

Homemade Praline

Delightful sprinkled over vanilla ice cream.

1 cup sugar
1 cup blanched almonds

In a cast-iron skillet, combine the sugar and almonds and cook over medium heat, stirring constantly, until golden brown. Pour into a lightly oiled pan and cool completely. When hard, place in blender and chop coarsely. Store in a covered jar in the refrigerator until ready to use.

Variation: Use hazelnuts instead of almonds.

Flambéed Dessert Sauce

A simple dessert will be enhanced with this excellent touch. Try it over poached pears, sponge cake, or ice cream.

4½ squares (4½ ounces) semisweet chocolate
¼ cup water
½ cup confectioner's sugar
¼ cup light cream
½ cup Grand Marnier

In the top of a double boiler over hot water, combine the chocolate and water until melted.

Beat in the sugar, cream and ¼ cup of the liqueur, and blend well. Remove from heat and pour into a pretty heatproof serving pan.

Heat the remaining ¼ cup of liqueur and pour slowly over the top of the sauce. Ignite and when the blue flame dies, spoon over selected dessert.

Makes about 1½ cups.

Brandied Mint Sauce

Delicious over coffee or vanilla ice cream.

¼ cup extra-strong coffee
¼ cup water
¼ cup sugar
4 squares (4 ounces) semisweet chocolate
1 square (1 ounce) bitter chocolate
2 tablespoons brandy
2 tablespoons white crème de menthe
1 teaspoon butter

In the top of a double boiler over hot water, combine the coffee, water, sugar, and chocolates, stirring until blended. Add the brandy, crème de menthe, and butter, and mix well.

Serve hot over selected ice cream.

Makes 1½ cups.

Whipped Cream with Suggested Liqueurs

Keep liqueur miniatures on hand rather than invest in the large size.

> 1 cup heavy cream
> ⅓ cup confectioner's sugar
> 2 tablespoons Tia Maria or Kahlua
> > *or*
> 1 tablespoon Grand Marnier, curaçao, or Triple Sec with 1 tablespoon grated orange zest
> > *or*
> 2 tablespoons crème de cacao with 2 teaspoons cocoa powder
> > *or*
> 2 tablespoons Framboise with ½ cup drained frozen raspberries or strawberries

Whip the cream until bubbly, then gradually add the sugar. Continue to beat until stiff.

Add the desired liqueur.

Use as topping.

Chocolate Whipped Cream

A luscious topping for plain cakes, ice cream, and molds.

> 2 cups whipping cream
> 2½ tablespoons crème de cacao
> 1 teaspoon Kahlua
> 1 tablespoon sugar

Beat the cream with the liqueurs and sugar until stiff. Refrigerate until ready to use.

Makes 2 cups.

Mexican Chocolate Sauce

A different taste admixture. Good served over cold pears with slivered almonds, or add chopped marrons and serve over plain cake, ice cream, or pudding.

4 squares (4 ounces) bitter chocolate
4 squares (4 ounces) sweet milk chocolate
2 cups plus 1 tablespoon of heavy cream
¼ cup honey
¼ cup sugar
1 teaspoon cinnamon

In a saucepan, melt the chocolates and the cream over low heat, stirring. Add the rest of the ingredients and cook, stirring, until desired consistency. Pour into 1-cup containers and freeze.

To use, add 1 tablespoon of heavy cream and reheat over low heat, stirring.

Makes 1½–2 pints.

Variation: Spoon slivered candied orange rind and orange liqueur on top of chocolate.

Toasted Coconut

A lovely topping for fruit desserts and whipped-cream-topped pies.

Grated coconut

Preheat oven to 350°F.

Sprinkle the grated coconut on a baking sheet and toast, stirring frequently, for about 7 minutes, until lightly browned.

BEVERAGES

Hot Chocolate Extravaganza
Mexican Hot Chocolate
Superb Hot Chocolate
Cold Bavarian Chocolate
Mocha Chocolate with Nutmeg
Spiced Mocha Chiller
Chocolate Cooler

Hot Chocolate Extravaganza

Serve this hot or cold for compliments anytime.

---

  2 tablespoons cocoa
  2 tablespoons sugar
    Pinch salt
  1 cup water
  3 cups milk
  ⅓ cup Kahlua
    Whipped cream for garnish, lightly sweetened

In a saucepan, stir together the cocoa, sugar, salt, and water until well mixed. Bring the mixture just to boiling over low heat, then stir constantly for 2 minutes more.

Add the milk and heat, then add the Kahlua.

Pour into cups or mugs and top with a dollop of whipped cream. **Serves 4.**

Mexican Hot Chocolate

A south-of-the-border specialty for cold weather.

4 squares (4 ounces) bitter chocolate, grated
½ cup boiling water
4 cups milk, scalded
2 cups light cream
7 tablespoons sugar
¼ teaspoon salt
  Pinch grated nutmeg
  Pinch grated allspice
2 teaspoons cinnamon, plus additional for garnish
2 eggs
2 teaspoons vanilla
½ cup whipping cream

In the top of a double boiler over hot but not boiling water, combine the chocolate and boiling water. When the chocolate is melted, beat it with a spoon, about 3 minutes, until smooth and blended. Stir in the hot milk, cream, 6 tablespoons of sugar, salt, and spices. Cook for 30 minutes over low heat, beating well every 10 minutes.

When ready to serve, beat the eggs with the vanilla until frothy. Add a little of the hot chocolate to the eggs, stir well, then gradually stir in the remainder of the chocolate. Beat well for about 3 minutes.

Serve at once.

Whip the cream with the remaining 1 tablespoon of sugar.

Pour the chocolate into cups and garnish with the whipped cream, sprinkled with cinnamon.

Serves 6–8.

Superb Hot Chocolate

For chocolate and orange aficionados, this is the one to try.

6 ounces semisweet chocolate bits
2 cups heavy cream
1 tablespoon Grand Marnier or more to taste
½ cup whipping cream
1 tablespoon sugar

In the top of a double boiler over hot but not boiling water, combine the chocolate and the cream. Heat to boiling, stirring.

When the chocolate is melted and the sauce well blended, remove from heat and stir in the liqueur.

Whip the cream with the sugar.

Pour the chocolate into mugs and top with whipped cream.
Serves 3–4.

Cold Bavarian Chocolate

A delicious departure from the ordinary chocolate drink. This recipe is per person.

1 ice cube
3 tablespoons Hershey's chocolate syrup
Extra-strong hot coffee
1 scoop vanilla ice cream
Whipped cream, lightly sweetened

Into a tall ice tea glass, place the ice cube and chocolate syrup. Fill ⅔ full with the coffee. Add a scoop of vanilla ice cream and a dollop of whipped cream.
Serves 1.

Mocha Chocolate with Nutmeg

A *lovely* beverage to serve on a frosty afternoon.

- 1 square (1 ounce) bitter chocolate, grated
- 4 tablespoons sugar
- 1½ cups milk
- Pinch salt
- 1½ cups extra-strong coffee
- ½ cup whipping cream
- Nutmeg

In the top of a double boiler over hot but not boiling water, combine the grated chocolate, 3 tablespoons of sugar, and ½ cup of milk. Cook, stirring occasionally, until the chocolate is melted. Add the salt and remaining milk, and cook over low heat for 10 minutes.

Beat with a rotary beater until frothy, then add the coffee slowly, beating constantly. Pour into a serving pitcher.

Whip the cream with the remaining 1 tablespoon of sugar.

Garnish with whipped cream and a dash of nutmeg.

Serves 4.

Spiced Mocha Chiller

A good thirst quencher for springtime.

6 squares (6 ounces) semisweet chocolate
½ teaspoon cinnamon
4 cups extra-strong hot coffee
Whipped cream for garnish, lightly sweetened

In the top of a double boiler over hot but not boiling water, melt the chocolate and blend in the cinnamon. Remove from heat and slowly blend the hot coffee into the chocolate mixture. Cool, then pour into ice tea glasses filled with ice.

To garnish, top with a dollop of whipped cream.
Serves 4–5.

Chocolate Cooler

A most welcome potable on a hot afternoon.

1 cup chocolate ice cream
1 cup club soda
3 tablespoons chocolate syrup
3 tablespoons heavy cream

Combine all the ingredients in an electric blender and blend for 30 seconds, until smooth. Chill thoroughly and serve in tall glasses.
Serves 2.

Index